The DUEL

GENERAL ALEXANDER HAMILTON

COLONEL AARON BURR

The DUEL

THE PARALLEL LIVES OF
ALEXANDER HAMILTON & AARON BURR

Judith St. George

speak

SPEAK
An imprint of Penguin Random House LLC
375 Hudson Street
New York, New York 10014

First published in the United States of America by Viking,
an imprint of Penguin Group (USA) Inc., 2009
Published by Speak, an imprint of Penguin Random House LLC, 2016

THE LIBRARY OF CONGRESS HAS CATALOGUED THE VIKING EDITION AS FOLLOWS:
St. George, Judith, 1931-
The duel : the parallel lives of Alexander Hamilton & Aaron Burr / Judith St. George.
p. cm.
ISBN 978-0-670-01124-7 (hc)
1. Burr-Hamilton Duel, Weehawken, N.J., 1804—Juvenile literature.
2. Burr, Aaron, 1756–1836—Juvenile literature.
3. Hamilton, Alexander, 1757–1804—Juvenile literature.
I. Title.
E302.6.H2S77 2009
973.4'6092—dc22
2009005660

Speak ISBN 978-0-425-28821-4

Book design by Sam Kim

Printed in the United States of America

5 7 9 10 8 6 4

To Sarah, Joe, Emily, and Hannah, with love

Contents

The DUEL

Prologue

At 4:00 A.M., after a good night's sleep on his library couch, the handsome, dark-eyed, dark-haired gentleman, known as the Colonel for his rank in the Revolutionary War, set out from his New York City home. On that rather cool summer morning of July 11, 1804, his good friend, William Van Ness, was with him.

By the time the two men boarded a barge at the foot of Canal Street, the sun had begun to rise. Four oarsmen rowed the Colonel and Van Ness across the clear blue Hudson River, already dotted with fishing boats. Ahead of them loomed the Palisades cliffs. Their destination? Weehawken, New Jersey. The purpose of their trip? A duel.

Arriving in Weehawken after almost two hours on the river, the Colonel and Van Ness climbed a footpath to a narrow, rocky ledge tucked into the New Jersey Palisades, some twenty feet above the river. Right away, they took off their coats and began to clear away underbrush and sticks.

Because the ledge was twenty-two paces long and eleven paces wide, it was the perfect dueling ground, in the perfect location. New York and New Jersey both banned dueling, but trees and tangled brush pretty much concealed the ledge. On the other hand, anyone standing on the lip of the ledge had a spectacular view of the Manhattan and New Jersey shorelines.

Another distinguished-looking gentleman, who had sandy hair and eyes so blue that they looked almost violet, rose at 3:00 A.M. in his New York City town house. Called the General because of his military rank when war with France had threatened in 1798, the gentleman sat down at his desk and began to write.

Sometime after four, two friends, Nathaniel Pendleton and Dr. David Hosack, arrived. Taking a carriage to a dock on the Hudson River, the men boarded a barge to be rowed three miles across the Hudson River to Weehawken.

Approaching the Weehawken shore just before seven, the little party saw four oarsmen and another barge on the beach. The Colonel and his second had already arrived! When the barge landed, Dr. Hosack stayed on the beach below with the oarsmen as the General and Pendleton hurried up the path.

When they saw each other, the duelists, Colonel Aaron Burr and General Alexander Hamilton, exchanged a formal greeting.

Chapter 1

ORPHANS: 1755–1769

From Alexander Hamilton's earliest days on the West Indian island of Nevis, he was an energetic, high-spirited, and unusually bright boy. Recognizing Alex's potential, his mother saw to it that he attended Jewish school. Because Alex was small and slight for his age, his teacher had him stand on a table to recite the Ten Commandments in Hebrew.

Looking back, Alex was grateful that he'd had a dedicated teacher who introduced him to his favorite subject, mathematics. And she started him on reading. Young Alex enjoyed reading more than anything he could think of.

Alex was born to Rachel Lavien and James Hamilton on January 11, 1755, on Nevis, a tiny British island in the Caribbean Sea. Rachel and James were not only down-and-out poor, they had also never married.

Rachel already had a husband, Johann Lavien. Though Rachel and Lavien had a son, their marriage was unhappy from the start. In 1750, while living on the island of St. Croix, Lavien had Rachel thrown in jail for being "twice guilty of adultery."

As soon as Rachel was released from jail, she ran away. Before long, she met up with James Hamilton, the ne'er-do-well son of a Scottish lord. Rachel and James had two children: James Jr., born in 1753, and Alex, born two years later. The illegitimate boys learned all too soon that they were politely called "natural children" by some people and not-so-politely called "obscene children" by others.

When their father was offered work in St. Croix in 1765, ten-year-old Alex and twelve-year-old James Jr. sailed with their parents to their new home. A beautiful eighty-four-square-mile island, St. Croix was set like a jewel in the Caribbean. With a population of ten thousand—nine thousand of whom were slaves—sugarcane was king. The sugarcane plantations produced what all the world wanted: sugar, molasses, and rum, which earned incredible riches for the white plantation owners.

But James wasn't a plantation owner. And like every other job he had held, success at his new job wasn't to be. "My father's affairs at a very early date went to wreck," Alexander Hamilton wrote years later.

Living on the edge in St. Croix's little town of Christiansted wasn't easy for Alex. Here he was with a father who was a failure and a mother who was the subject of gossip and disdain for having been in jail. And it seemed to Alex that everywhere he went, people flaunted their wealth. Alex's life became even harder when his father announced to his family in 1766 that he was leaving them and wouldn't be back.

But Rachel was a survivor, and she began to sell groceries out of their tiny St. Croix home for a local merchant, Nicholas Cruger. Alex was a survivor, too, and he pitched in. Although he was only eleven, he took over his mother's accounts and bookkeeping. Mathematics was his special talent.

Because selling groceries wasn't enough to keep them going, Alex hired out to do bookkeeping at Nicholas Cruger's successful import-export business. For sure, he'd rather have been in school, but he was only free to go from time to time. At least he met his best friend there, Ned Stevens, with whom he took "vows of eternal friendship."

Surrounded by magnificent estates and elegant homes, Alex's family struggled to make ends meet. The charm and beauty of St. Croix's sandy beaches, tropical sea breezes, and azure Caribbean waters were lost on them.

Then Rachel fell ill with a high fever, and her recovery became the boys' only concern. She grew sicker and weaker by the day. On February 19, 1768, Rachel died on the family's only bed, side by side with grief-stricken twelve-year-old Alex, who had been laid low by fever too.

With their father out of the picture and their mother dead, Alex and James were now orphans. What a long walk it was to the St. Croix graveyard for the two boys. No doubt they wept behind their black veils as they followed their mother's hearse to her grave. And the brothers were left with nothing of Rachel's to remember her by. The St. Croix courts awarded her belongings to Rachel's adult son by Lavien, whom she hadn't seen for seventeen years. Later, however, Alex was given her books, which he treasured.

Alex and James's situation didn't improve when the courts named their cousin, Peter Lytton, to be their guardian. The two boys were sure that Peter Lytton cared nothing for them, and he didn't. Because he was a failure in business, Peter had little money, certainly no money to spend on his young cousins. At least Peter's father, Uncle James, pitched in to help keep a roof over the boys' heads and food on their table.

But in July 1769, Alex was dealt another blow when Peter Lytton committed suicide. A month later, Uncle James Lytton died too. Alex and James's only hope was that they had been left some money, no matter how little. But they received nothing.

Alex and James were alone and homeless.

Alexander Hamilton, who had endured his father's disappearance and his mother's death, as well as town gossip and public humiliation, had learned to hold his head high. Never one to dwell on the past, Alex would always be a take-charge person, ready to move forward. And that was what he would do now.

Unlike Alexander Hamilton's humble arrival into the world, Aaron Burr's birth on February 6, 1756, in Newark, New Jersey, was celebrated by a large and distinguished family that had arrived in America more than a hundred years before.

Aaron's mother, Esther, was one of eleven children of the famous clergyman, the Reverend Jonathan Edwards. Aaron's father, Aaron Burr, Sr., was the pastor of the First Presbyterian Church in Newark *and* president of the College of New Jersey, later known as Princeton University. Aaron and his family were British citizens, as were most Americans in the 1750s. (Because Alexander Hamilton's parents had both been British citizens, he was a British citizen, too.)

In December 1756, Aaron's parents moved with ten-month-old Aaron and his two-and-a-half-year-old sister, Sally, to the college president's newly built house in Princeton, New Jersey. But when Aaron was nineteen months old, he became aware that something was terribly wrong. And something was—Aaron's father, who had been gravely ill with intermittent fever, died.

Left to raise Aaron and Sally alone, Esther Burr wrote to a friend that Aaron was smarter and handsomer than his older sister, but "not so good tempered." As dearly as she loved her son, early on she recognized his strong personality, calling him "a resolute boy" and "a little dirty Noisy Boy . . . very sly and mischievous."

"Dirty" and "noisy" didn't matter when young Aaron fell critically ill six weeks after his father died. But "resolute" did. "My little son has been sick with the slow fever, and has been brought to the brink of death," Esther lamented. Perhaps young Aaron's resolute and determined character was what pulled him through, even at that young age.

The following February, Aaron's grandfather, the Reverend Jonathan Edwards, arrived in Princeton to take over as president of the college. But a smallpox epidemic was sweeping across New Jersey. To prevent the disease, Dr. William Shippen, a good friend, vaccinated the Edwards family members. But Jonathan Edwards developed the dreaded "secondary fever" from the vaccination and died only a month after his arrival.

Less than a month later, Aaron's heartbroken mother, who was still mourning the death of both her husband and her father, died, too. Though she was "seemingly without any disease," Dr. Shippen's smallpox vaccination had probably caused her death.

A confused and unhappy Aaron was only two when he was orphaned. Explanations and empty phrases meant nothing. All he knew, or cared about, was that his mother and father were both mysteriously gone.

At least Aaron wasn't homeless the way orphaned Alex Hamilton had been. But a new home meant that Aaron and his sister, Sally, were uprooted from everything familiar when Dr. William Shippen scooped them up and took them back to Philadelphia to live with him.

Five months later, Grandmother Sarah Edwards arrived in Philadelphia to take Aaron and Sally back with her to Massachusetts. It never happened. Grandmother Edwards fell ill with dysentery. Though Dr. Shippen did his best, she died while still in Philadelphia.

Incredibly, in little more than a year, death had snatched away every person whom Aaron had loved and counted on: his father, mother, both Edwards grandparents, and even his great-grandfather, Daniel Burr. In an almost unimaginable roll call of deaths, Aaron and Sally were more than orphaned. They were doubly orphaned.

To give the Shippens credit, for two years, Aaron and Sally had a loving home in the Shippens' handsome brick house, and Aaron became fond of them. But all that changed again when four-year-old Aaron and almost seven-year-old Sally became the legal wards of their grandparents' oldest son, Timothy Edwards. Aaron didn't know twenty-one-year-old Uncle Timothy or his bride, Rhoda Ogden, now his Aunt Rhoda. It didn't matter that they were strangers. The court order had to be obeyed.

When Uncle Timothy and Aunt Rhoda arrived in Philadelphia to pick up their two wards and take them back to Elizabethtown, New Jersey, Aaron's belongings were all packed. It was time to say good-bye to the Shippens and the only life he'd known for two years—a sad moment.

Aaron had trouble fitting into his new home. Because Uncle Timothy was also guardian to a number of younger brothers and sisters who had been orphaned, too, the Elizabethtown house was bursting at the seams. And Uncle Timothy and Aunt Rhoda added a new baby to the household almost every year.

Esther Burr had called her son resolute. To keep from getting lost in the shuffle, he had to be. When four-year-old Aaron "took offense" at his Uncle Timothy, he resolutely ran away . . . briefly. Aaron next took offense at the "prim behavior" of an elderly guest. From his perch in a cherry tree, he pelted her with cherries as she strolled in the Edwards family orchard.

At ten, Aaron made a more serious run for freedom, signing up as cabin boy on a ship docked in New York. When Uncle Timothy finally tracked him down, Aaron clambered up the topgallant mast and wouldn't budge until his uncle promised not to whip him "like a sack" the way he once had.

Aaron was not only resolute, but he was also resourceful in finding ways to entertain himself. He sailed his skiff and hunted and fished in Elizabethtown's nearby swamps with his best friend, Matt Ogden, Aunt Rhoda's younger brother. The two boys even ventured out into the Arthur Kill Channel to catch saltwater fish.

Despite all of his responsibilities, Uncle Timothy made sure that Aaron and Sally were educated. Tapping Reeve came into their lives as a tutor—and ended up marrying Sally when she was seventeen. Aaron studied at

Barber's Academy, where Uncle Timothy served on the Board of Visitors. Like Alex Hamilton, Aaron was unusually bright and excelled in all his studies.

In 1767, eleven-year-old Aaron applied to the College of New Jersey. But he was small and thin for his age, and, with his delicate oval face and large, dark brown eyes under a lock of dark hair, he looked even younger than eleven. It took only one quick glance for the examiners to turn Aaron down.

To think that the examiners had rejected him, the son and grandson of College of New Jersey presidents! Well, he'd show them.

Aaron devoted his next two years to serious study so that he could pass the exams with flying colors. Never had Aaron Burr been more resolute.

Chapter 2

STUDENTS: 1769–1773

Thirteen–year–old Aaron Burr did so well on his College of New Jersey exams that he was accepted as a second-year student. As soon as he arrived at the college, he dug in and tackled his courses. He'd prove to those examiners that he could perfectly well have started college as a third-year student.

In the mornings, Aaron got up before five to study by candlelight. During the day he studied every spare moment and didn't close his books until nine at night. Sometimes in the afternoons, he found it hard to keep his mind on his studies. That wouldn't do. He'd skip the noonday dinner, or if he ate, he'd eat just a little, a routine he followed whenever he was under pressure for the rest of his life. Whatever his methods, they worked. He got such high grades after his first examinations that he could let his studies pretty much coast for his last two years.

It wasn't as if Aaron's college routine weren't tough enough. All one hundred students lived and went to classes in Nassau Hall, a handsome three-story stone building. A bell woke the boys up at 5 A.M., except for those, like Aaron, who were already up. Half an hour later, a servant pounded on every door. If no one answered, he'd go in and drag the student out of bed.

Morning prayers began the day. Next came study time, breakfast, and then four hours of classes. Dinner was at one, with two free hours before another study period. Supper was at five o'clock, followed by more study and evening prayers, with candles snuffed out at nine, like it or not. Because neither the campus nor Princeton village had much to offer, free time usually meant hanging out with friends. Nassau Hall, a kitchen house, an outhouse, a fire engine shed, and the president's house, where Aaron had lived briefly as an infant, made up the entire campus. The village of Princeton itself was a one-street hamlet.

Considering how hard Aaron worked and how little spare time he had, he was instantly popular. And because of his age and small size, he was affectionately known as "Little Burr." Even at thirteen, he had a magnetism that charmed many of his classmates into becoming lifelong friends.

One of Aaron's friends, William Paterson, who had graduated from the college six years before, lived nearby and was always interested in getting to know and help promising students. Aaron Burr was nothing if not promising. In a letter to Aaron, William Paterson wrote: "To do you any little services in my power will afford me great satisfaction, and I hope you will . . . call upon me whenever you think you can."

James Madison, a future president of the United States, was a College of

New Jersey student too. Aaron and James knew each other, but they were never friends, or even friendly. They first rubbed up against one another when they belonged to rival literary societies.

Aaron joined the Cliosophic Society, founded by his friend William Paterson, while James Madison was a founder of the other literary club, the American Whig Society. Members of both clubs, which each met in Nassau Hall, spent a lot of their time sending insulting poems back and forth. Since the clubs were literary societies, their members also read aloud papers they'd written. In one of Aaron's papers, he pointed out that dueling was a foolish business. It was a paper that would come back to haunt him years later.

Even though Aaron tended to slack off his last two years, he was so bright that his grades were respectable. He wasn't at the top of his class, but he wasn't at the bottom either. His professors awarded him first honors for "reading the English language" and for "answering questions on Orthography," a fancy eighteenth-century word for spelling. He received second honors for "reading the Latin and Greek languages" in the original.

Sixteen-year-old Aaron's graduation address in September 1772 was "Building Castles in the Air." Oddly enough, he advised his audience not to waste time dreaming of future fame and success. It was advice that he ignored for the rest of his life.

As it turned out, Aaron didn't even follow his own advice after graduation. Uncle Timothy Edwards had invested Aaron's inheritance wisely, which meant he had enough money to drift and dream for a while. Aaron stayed on in the hamlet of Princeton for a year, although he returned to

Elizabethtown from time to time to hunt and fish with his friend Matt Ogden. By now, Aaron had a newfound fondness for girls as well as becoming a master at the art of flirting.

During his year off, Aaron did a lot of reading and mulling over what to do with the rest of his life. He didn't have many choices. As an educated young gentleman, he could choose from only a few professions such as law or medicine, or he could follow his father, grandfather, and great-grandfather into the ministry.

But making a commitment was hard. When Aaron was two, he had lost everything and everyone he had ever loved or counted on. As he grew up, he found it easier to back off without committing himself to anything until he could figure out what offered the greatest and safest reward. And choosing one profession meant rejecting other possibilities that might prove worthier in the long run.

A college friend, Samuel Spring, reminded Aaron that his parents had wanted him to be a minister. "Remember," Samuel wrote, "that was the prayer of your dear father and mother."

Yes, true enough. All right, he'd give the ministry a try.

In the fall of 1773, seventeen-year-old Aaron began studying under the Reverend Dr. Joseph Bellamy in Connecticut. Dr. Bellamy was a taskmaster who insisted that his students defend doubts or any objections they might have to his religious teachings. Aaron plunged in and studied hard, though he wrote to his sister Sally that he was a dawdler, or, as he put it, "I am pretty much of a quiddle."

After only a few months, Aaron grew restless. Maybe by questioning Dr. Bellamy's religious teachings, he'd raised doubts in his own mind. Or maybe he missed having a fun social life. With a touch of envy, that winter he'd written to his sister that he'd seen "six Slayloads of Bucks and Bells from Woodberry, and a happier Company I believe there never was . . . they were drinking Cherry-Rum."

Whatever his reasons, Aaron realized he'd made the wrong choice. The ministry wasn't for him. But what was? He didn't know.

What a lucky break for orphaned and homeless Alexander Hamilton! The parents of his best friend, Ned Stevens, took him into their St. Croix home. Not only were fourteen-year-old Alex and Ned best friends, but they looked alike. They were both small, slender, and frail, with the same Scottish sandy hair and fair, rosy complexion. Their personalities were the same, too: quick, clever, high-spirited, and bright. Even as adults, they were mistaken for brothers.

Could they possibly be related? Because of their amazing resemblance, there were rumors that Ned's father, Thomas Stevens, and not James Hamilton, was Alex's father. It was never proved one way or the other, but if he was, that would make the boys half brothers, reason enough for them to look alike.

Alex's older brother, James, found a home, too. He apprenticed to an elderly carpenter with whom he boarded. Alex and James had never had much in common. When they went their separate ways, for all intents and purposes, that was the end of their relationship.

Luckily Alex still had his bookkeeping job at Nicholas Cruger's import-export business, where his financial skills blossomed. He tracked freight, charted courses for ships, learned to calculate prices in foreign currencies, and kept the company books in his clear, elegant handwriting. What Alex liked least about the import-export business was dealing with the chained, "sickly and thin" slaves arriving from Africa for sale to the wealthy owners of St. Croix's sugar plantations. As a firsthand witness to the brutal slave trade, Alex developed a lifelong hatred of slavery.

Though Alex was learning a lot, he wanted something more. He wanted out of St. Croix. Why should he stay on a tiny island where his family background earned him nothing but scorn? Even worse, St. Croix offered no opportunity to gain the fame and fortune he dreamed about.

Alex described how he felt in a letter to Ned Stevens, who had recently left St. Croix to attend college in New York City. Fourteen-year-old Alex admitted that he was so ambitious that he was willing to risk his life— though not his character—to make a name for himself. Maybe the military could bring him the honor and recognition he craved. He ended his letter: "I wish there was a war. Alex. Hamilton."

In his eagerness to leave St. Croix, Alex had one winning asset—his strong drive to educate and better himself. But it took a newcomer to recognize Alex's brilliance and determination. Soon after the Reverend Hugh Knox arrived in St. Croix as pastor of the Presbyterian church, he met Alex. Right away, Knox was impressed, describing his young friend as having an "ambition to excel."

Hugh Knox opened his library to Alex, encouraged him to write poetry, and launched him on a solid classical education. Because the Reverend Aaron Burr, Sr., had been Knox's professor in college, and had ordained him to the ministry, Alex no doubt first heard the name "Aaron Burr" from Hugh Knox.

In the end, however, a monster hurricane that struck St. Croix in 1772 became Alex's means of escape. He described the hurricane's devastation in a dramatic letter to his father. Although it had been six years since Alex had seen his father, who now lived on a distant Caribbean island, he tried to stay in touch. He wrote: "What horror and destruction . . . the roaring of the sea and wind . . . fiery meteors flying about . . . perpetual lightning . . . the crash of falling houses . . . the ear-piercing shrieks of the distressed." He showed the letter to Knox, who urged him to send it to the St. Croix newspaper, which had already printed some of Alex's poems. The anonymous letter caused its own excitement. Even St. Croix's governor demanded to know its author.

Hugh Knox took advantage of the acclaim and began a fund for Alex to travel to America for a college education. College! Maybe college was a possibility after all. Nicholas Cruger jumped onboard, as did Alex's guardian, Thomas Stevens, and other St. Croix businessmen, many from wealthy New York and New Jersey families.

That fall, a very happy seventeen-year-old Alexander Hamilton boarded a ship bound for Boston. He had no regrets at leaving St. Croix, no desire to speak of St. Croix ever again, and, above all, no wish to return. But his ship caught fire at sea. After all this effort to reach America, he might not even make it! Alex wasn't going to put up with that. He lined up with the crew to pass endless buckets of water to the firefighters. With the fire finally out, the ship limped into Boston Harbor, three weeks after leaving St. Croix.

Because his letters of introduction were to prominent New York and New Jersey businessmen, Alex left Boston and headed for New York City. He was also anxious to visit his friend Ned Stevens at King's College in New York. Alex had another good reason for hightailing it to New York: that was where his scholarship fund was waiting.

Armed with his letters of introduction, eighteen-year-old Alex enrolled at Hugh Knox's old school, Barber's Academy, in Elizabethtown, New Jersey. With that, the connection between Alexander Hamilton and Aaron Burr was made, never to be broken. While living in Elizabethtown with his uncle Timothy, Aaron Burr had also gone to Barber's Academy to prepare for college.

When Alex arrived in Elizabethtown, seventeen-year-old Aaron Burr, who had graduated from the College of New Jersey the year before, was also in Elizabethtown visiting his friend Matt Ogden.

It was possible that in a town of only four hundred homes Alex and Aaron would run into each other, maybe boating on the town's inlets or fishing in the Arthur Kill. A more likely meeting place was in the drawing rooms of Elizabethtown's prominent citizens whose doors had always been open to Aaron because of his family connections. Those doors were now opened to Alex by his letters of introduction. Handsome and well-spoken, he fit in easily. Even better, no one questioned his background. It didn't take Alex long to decide that within this charmed circle of American aristocrats was where he belonged.

Aaron Burr had attended Barber's Academy to catch up on his College of New Jersey requirements. Six years later, Alex attended Barber's Academy for the same reason, to catch up on *his* Greek, Latin, French, history, geography, and mathematics so that he, too, could enter the College of New Jersey.

But, like Aaron Burr, who first applied when he was eleven, Alex was rejected. Most students began college at fourteen or fifteen. Already eighteen, Alex insisted that he be allowed to study at his own pace and graduate as soon as possible. Absolutely not, the examiners told him. He would have to complete college in the usual four years. Well then, so be it, Alex decided. If they didn't want him, then he didn't want them.

Alex wasn't used to failure, and the College of New Jersey was part of his long-range plan. Ambitious and totally focused on following the route to success that he'd mapped out for himself, Alex was stopped short. Well, somehow, some way, he'd get past this unexpected bump in the road.

Chapter 3

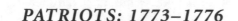

PATRIOTS: 1773–1776

Alexander Hamilton wasn't one to waste time making up his mind. If the College of New Jersey wouldn't let him take courses at his own speed, then he'd go to King's College with his friend Ned Stevens.

Alex enrolled at King's College in New York City, later known as Columbia University, in the fall of 1773. At eighteen, he had reached his full height, about five foot seven. Slender, with a fair complexion, auburn hair, and intensely blue eyes, he was an energetic and self-assured young man.

Hamilton found New York to be a bustling, fast-moving city of about twenty-five thousand with such a mixed population that more than fifteen languages were heard on the streets. Although King's College had the same kinds of courses as the College of New Jersey, it was smaller, with some twenty students. The whole college was housed in a three-story building.

Alex liked one big difference. At King's, he was allowed to set his own schedule. And he was a fast learner. He studied hard, raced through all the books he could get his hands on, and remembered almost everything he read. Like Aaron Burr, he mastered Greek and Latin.

Also, like Aaron Burr, Alex made friends easily, hitting it off right away with his roommate, Robert Troup, who was an orphan, too. Alex, though, was a leader, while Robert tended to be a follower. Several years later, Robert became friends with another self-confident young man—Aaron Burr, who teased Robert by calling him "that great fat fellow."

Alex had barely begun King's College, when, on December 16, a Boston mob dressed as Indians dumped more than three hundred casks of British tea into Boston Harbor to protest the tax the British had slapped on their tea coming into the colonies. Although Alex had left St. Croix only the year before, he was already calling America "my country." Drawn to the American cause, Alex jumped to the defense of what was called the Boston Tea Party in an article he wrote anonymously for a New York newspaper.

Soon after, eighteen-year-old Alex mounted the platform at a rally of the Sons of Liberty, a militant group of American rebels. There he gave an off-the-cuff speech condemning the British for punishing Bostonians with higher taxes. If no one opposed the British, he said, "fraud, power, and the most odious oppression will rise triumphant over right, justice, social happiness, and freedom." Looking even younger than he was, Alex, with his amazing eloquence, gained an instant reputation as a rebel spokesman.

Alex thrived on controversy. For the next two years, he and a pro-British clergyman, Samuel Seabury, waged war with essays and letters published in a New York newspaper. Alex predicted—correctly—that there would be a war with Great Britain that would be fought in skirmishes rather than pitched battles. He also predicted—correctly—that

France and Spain would come to America's aid. After winning the war, he concluded, America's economic power would surpass Great Britain's. Readers of the brilliant unsigned essays never dreamed that their author was only a college student.

American protest came to a head on April 18, 1775, when Massachusetts farmers, called Minutemen, defeated eight hundred British troops at the battles of Lexington and Concord. At the news, both New York City and the country were in an uproar.

Spurred on by the victory, Alex and Robert Troup joined a newly formed militia company known as Hearts of Oak. Robert reported that Alex drilled faithfully every day, and was "constant in his attendance and very ambitious of improvement." At the same time, Alex kept up with his college work, continued to write articles for the newspaper, and studied war strategy and military tactics.

Three weeks after Lexington and Concord, a mob of rebels stormed King's College to tar and feather the college's president, Dr. Myles Cooper, an outspoken supporter of British rule. When Alex got word of the plot, he rushed to the president's house. Taking a stand on the front steps, he argued that to tar and feather the president would "injure and disgrace the glorious cause of liberty." Because Alex's patriotism was well known, the protesters backed off.

Alex had shown great courage. The crowd could have turned against him. Or he could have lost his reputation as a dedicated patriot. But Alex loathed mob rule, and much as he was willing to fight for what he believed was right, he also had a sense of personal honor and respect for law and order.

That August, the British warship *Asia* anchored in New York Harbor.

Once again Alex jumped into the fray. To save the twenty-four cannon that guarded the tip of Manhattan, Alex and fifteen other King's College students began hauling the heavy cannon by rope to a safe location. To stop them, the *Asia* let loose with fierce shelling. Terrified New Yorkers ran from their homes as students, including Alex, fired back. Despite the constant British bombardment, Alex and his classmates rescued all the cannon.

On that same day in August 1775, King George III in England proclaimed that the American resistance had to be put down. War loomed. That did it for Alex. After two and a half years of college, he was through. He wanted action, not Latin and Greek. He enlisted in the army.

In March 1776, twenty-one-year-old Alex Hamilton was commissioned captain of an artillery company in New York City. Some of the sixty-eight men under his command couldn't read or write, and certainly none of them looked like soldiers. Captain Hamilton wasn't about to put up with that. He bought uniforms and equipment for his men and even lent them money from his St. Croix fund. "Smart dress is essential," he said. "When not attended to, the soldier is exposed to ridicule and humiliation."

Hamilton ceaselessly drilled and trained his men. He was a strict leader, but because he was fair-minded, his men respected and liked him. Perfectionist that he was, Hamilton soon had his company in tip-top shape. "It was esteemed the most beautiful model of discipline in the whole army," declared Robert Troup.

That April George Washington arrived in New York City to prepare for a possible British attack. Three hundred British ships carrying thirty-two thousand British fighting men rode at anchor just south of the city. In contrast, Washington had some twenty thousand inexperienced soldiers and no navy at all.

New York City itself had turned into a ghost town, with a fifth of its citizens having fled. Houses were boarded up, lead taken off roofs to make bullets, and trees cut down for firewood.

Under orders, Captain Hamilton instructed his men to build a small, temporary outpost near the southern tip of Manhattan that was called Bayard's Hill Redoubt. On July 2, 1776, Hamilton and his men watched in dismay from rooftops as a forest of masts flying the British flag sailed into New York's Upper Bay. With no opposition, many thousands of red-coated soldiers disembarked on nearby Staten Island.

Just two days later, when defeat stared the thirteen colonies in the face, the Second Continental Congress in Philadelphia voted to adopt the Declaration of Independence. All ties with Great Britain were cut. The die was cast.

Twenty-one-year-old Captain Alexander Hamilton, who would rather act than wait, had no choice but to wait for the British to attack. He'd drilled and trained his men. They were battle-ready, and so was he.

BURR

By the end of 1773, seventeen-year-old Aaron Burr had decided for sure that he didn't want to be a clergyman. But he didn't want to be a doctor either. Law was all that was left. Undecided about his next step, Aaron wrote his uncle Timothy. Should he study law with his sister Sally's husband, Tapping Reeve, or with his uncle Pierpont Edwards? "I would have you act your pleasure," Uncle Timothy replied.

But Aaron was in no hurry. He dawdled until May before heading for his sister's house in Litchfield, Connecticut. But even after he began to study law, his heart wasn't in it. Instead of describing his studies, his letters to his friend Matt Ogden were full of gossip about the enchanting Litchfield girls.

Matt responded enthusiastically: "I read with pleasure your love intrigues."

At eighteen, Aaron already had quite a reputation as a ladies' man. Even as he began to take serious notice of the rising tension between the New England colonies and Great Britain, he courted the Litchfield girls, most of whom never forgot the handsome young Aaron Burr.

As Aaron was drawn more and more into the rebel cause, like Alexander Hamilton, he began to study military history and battle tactics. In 1774, Aaron described how "a mob of several hundred persons . . . tore down the house of a man who was suspected of being unfriendly to the liberties of the people."

And when Aaron heard about the battles of Lexington and Concord, for once he made an instant decision, just as Alex Hamilton had. But whereas Alex Hamilton had joined a part-time militia unit, Aaron wrote Matt that the two of them should enlist as full-time soldiers in the new Continental Army that was assembling in Cambridge, Massachusetts.

Not now, Matt answered. He was too busy.

But in June, news of a bloody battle on Breed's Hill, across the bay from Boston, fired up Aaron, and he traveled to New Jersey to get Matt going. Alexander Hamilton dropped out of college to enlist in the army.

So, too, did Aaron Burr walk away from his law studies without a backward glance.

Aaron was soon on his way to Cambridge with Matt, who carried a congressman's letter recommending him for military service. The letter also recommended Aaron Burr, a "young Gentleman . . . the only Son of our old worthy Friend President Burr. He is on the same errand in the hopes of improving his youth to the advantage of his country."

But when Aaron and Matt reached Cambridge, they found the new commander in chief of the Continental army, George Washington, coping with chaos. Some sixteen thousand volunteers had enlisted, but they were mostly independent-minded New England farmers who balked at any military routine. Filthy tents and huts were scattered everywhere. Artillery and ammunition were in such short supply that a face-off with the British would have been a disaster.

Aaron, who was disgusted, took to his bed with what he called a fever. But when he heard that the army was planning an attack on British-held Canada, he quickly recovered. General Richard Montgomery was ordered to capture Montreal, while Colonel Benedict Arnold was ordered to take Quebec City.

That was more like it.

Aaron couldn't wait to volunteer. But Matt Ogden, who had already signed up, tried to discourage him. The 350-mile hike to Canada was through almost impenetrable wilderness. Matt was husky and muscular, while nineteen-year-old Aaron, at not quite five foot seven, was the Little Burr of his school days. He was still slender and frail, with the same dark hair and dark brown, almost black eyes.

Because Aaron couldn't be stopped, on September 13, the two "Gentlemen volunteers"—Cadet Burr and Cadet Ogden—began their march to Quebec under the command of Colonel Benedict Arnold.

In a letter to his sister, Sally, Aaron described his "traveling Dress" as "a pr of Boots . . . Woolen Trousers . . . a short double breasted Jacket . . . a short coat . . . a blanket . . . small round hat with a snap-up brim . . . a Tommahawk, Gun, Bayonet, etc." He was ready for action.

During the six-week journey to Canada, Colonel Benedict Arnold didn't bother with discipline. It was each man for himself. Some hiked, while others paddled up the Kennebec River in tublike boats called bateaux. The men had to cross frozen streams, slog through swamps, climb mountains in the snow, and hack through dense forests. When Aaron's bateau plunged over a twenty-foot waterfall, one man drowned and Aaron and the others barely made it to shore. Starving men shot dogs for food. Three companies turned back.

Not Aaron Burr. He stayed good-humored and healthy. As a skilled helmsman, he had handled heavy boats in rough seas while fishing. He was used to miserable conditions on his hunting trips in the New Jersey swamps. And his years of disciplined fasting at college stood him in good stead when there was little food.

Of the eleven hundred men who started out, only seven hundred and fifty crossed the St. Lawrence River to land south of Quebec City in Canada. Built on the side of a cliff and guarded by the strongest fortress in North America, Quebec was manned by eighteen hundred men.

The American siege of the city began.

Impressed by Aaron's remarkable endurance in the wilderness, Colonel Arnold ordered him to travel upriver to Montreal and accompany General Richard Montgomery back to Quebec. The plan was that Montgomery, who had captured Montreal, would supply Arnold with arms and clothing and a reinforcement of some three hundred soldiers. In a letter to Montgomery, Arnold praised Aaron: "He is a young gentleman of much life and activity, and has acted with great spirit and resolution on our fatiguing march."

General Montgomery was impressed by Aaron Burr, too. The aristocratic young cadet met Montgomery's standards of a gentleman soldier. By the time they reached Quebec, Montgomery had appointed Aaron his aide-de-camp and promoted him to captain.

In a howling blizzard on December 31, 1775, the American troops split up to attack Quebec on two fronts. Against the advice of Captain Burr and other officers, General Montgomery marched in the forefront of his division. The first barricade was no problem, but ahead was a fortified blockhouse. At the Americans' approach, musketeers inside opened fire, with gunners lighting the cannon.

A volley of grapeshot struck Montgomery a mortal blow and killed two of his aides. Burr caught the wounded general as he fell. Of those in the front line, only Burr and a French guide survived. Captain Burr urged the troops forward, but a higher-ranking officer ordered a retreat.

Burr refused to leave. General Montgomery deserved a proper military burial. Burr lifted the general to his narrow shoulders, but he didn't have the strength to make it through the deep snow. He had no choice but to lay the body down and flee to escape capture.

Colonel Arnold, leading the other attack, was also driven back. Like Montgomery, he, too, was shot, but his was a leg wound and not fatal.

For the rest of the winter, Burr and more than five hundred soldiers camped out in snow-and-ice forts, laying siege to Quebec, at the same time doing their best to survive a smallpox epidemic. Burr was again serving under Benedict Arnold, now a general. But he disliked Arnold intensely as a mean-spirited leader who refused to share hardships with his men

Burr wrote to Sally that he was "dirty, ragged, moneyless and friendless." He was hardly friendless. Friends and strangers alike wrote to congratulate him on his heroism in the Quebec fighting, with such praise as "brave . . . honorable . . . glorious . . . gallant . . . intrepid."

Before the winter was out, Matt Ogden left for home to join the First New Jersey Battalion. Even though Aaron felt forsaken, Matt was still his best friend. "If my heart, my life, or my fortune can assist you, it is yours," he wrote Matt.

But Matt had hardly forsaken Aaron. Just the opposite. Stopping in the capital of Philadelphia, where Captain Burr's courageous stand was all the talk, Matt arranged a new and prestigious assignment for his friend.

The first Burr knew something was up was when he was ordered to leave Canada for New York City. He wrote to his sister in May that he was headed south "on public business." It wasn't until Burr, now twenty and newly promoted to major, reached Albany, New York, that he heard he'd been honored with an appointment to George Washington's personal staff.

In June of 1776, Major Burr reported to General Washington in New York at his headquarters, an impressive mansion called Richmond Hill. But Washington, who apparently took an instant dislike to Burr, never accepted him into his "family," as he called his personal staff. Was it because Burr, with his illustrious Burr-and-Edwards heritage, plus four years of college, had an air of superiority? Or perhaps Burr was too ready to give unwanted advice. Maybe Washington, who expected undying loyalty from his "family," was aware that Burr was bored at headquarters.

Burr *was* bored. Still heady from the praise showered on him for his Quebec exploits, he craved action, not pushing papers at a desk. He was no clerk!

Burr wrote to John Hancock, an old family friend, to confess that he was unhappy and thinking of resigning from the army. Hancock urged him not to. There was a staff opening in New York City with General Israel Putnam, Washington's second in command, if Burr wanted it.

Burr definitely wanted it. After only ten days on Washington's staff, he left Richmond Hill and reported to General Putnam.

As General Putnam's aid-de-camp, Burr lived with the Putnam family in a large brick house that also served as New York headquarters. Nicknamed Old Put, fifty-eight-year-old Israel Putnam was an outspoken, warmhearted, battle-experienced New Englander. Major Aaron Burr took to him right away and before long was privately calling him "my good old general."

Now this was more like it.

Chapter 4

HEROES: 1776–1781

Major Aaron Burr certainly wasn't bored at General Israel Putnam's headquarters. Soon after he reported for duty in July 1776, beautiful Margaret Moncrieffe, a British officer's daughter, also arrived at the house. Although Margaret had been in custody as a prisoner of war, she'd been released and assigned to live with the Putnams. The dashing twenty-year-old Major Burr swept Margaret off her feet.

Margaret enjoyed painting New York City scenes from the roof of headquarters. Tradition says that Burr was admiring Margaret's paintings one day when he noticed she had painted in all the American fortifications. A British spy! That was the end of the romance. And it was the end of Margaret's visit. She was shipped back to her father. But, oh, how she missed the young American officer she thought of as "the conqueror of my soul."

Burr may have missed Margaret, but a war was on and he was in it. That August, General Putnam sent Burr to Long Island to check up on America's military defenses and report back. Burr's report wasn't good: the British "will hem us in, and totally cut off all communication, after which they will have their own fun."

Burr was right on target.

On August 27, General Putnam's force of nine thousand fighting men fought some twenty thousand British and Hessian soldiers on Long Island. Outmanned and outgunned in a one-day battle, Old Put's soldiers retreated in a hurry. Thanks to General Washington's efforts, the American survivors were all ferried safely across the East River to Manhattan under cover of a heavy fog that had conveniently blown in.

Three weeks later, thirteen thousand British troops landed on Manhattan's East Side. With most of the army holed up in the wilderness of Harlem Heights, General Putnam, with his loyal aide, Major Burr, was ordered to hold off the British with only four thousand men. They didn't last long. In another hasty retreat, Old Put ordered his force to head up the East Side toward Harlem Heights. No, no, Burr protested, fleeing up the East Side would lead them into the waiting arms of the British.

If General Putnam trusted any soldier's judgment, that soldier was Major Burr. Old Put reversed his command and ordered a double-quick march up the West Side. Encountering only sporadic gunfire from the British, the soldiers safely joined the rest of the army on Harlem Heights.

Only General Gold Silliman's brigade at Bayard's Hill Redoubt, where Alexander Hamilton was stationed, was still in danger. Old Put ordered Burr to ride down and escort the brigade back to Harlem Heights. But when Burr arrived, Silliman wouldn't budge. Burr galloped away, only to turn back to report he'd just received new orders. Abandon your post. Now! Silliman fell for the trick, and Burr led the brigade back to the safety of Harlem Heights.

Although Burr never claimed he had saved Alexander Hamilton from capture or death, more than likely he had. Because Burr was always hungry for praise and recognition, he was annoyed that Washington didn't give him credit for rescuing an entire brigade at the risk of his own life. Never a fan of Washington, Burr accused his commander in chief of intentionally overlooking his heroism.

After serving under Old Put for a year, Burr was promoted to lieutenant colonel. Burr had once written to Matt Ogden that "expectations of promotion, I have not the least." But he was unhappy that Washington had once again bypassed him. In an icy letter to his commander in chief, Major Burr wrote that the "late date of my appointment" came after newer and younger officers had been promoted.

Washington never replied to the colonel's insolent letter.

In July, twenty-one-year-old Burr was assigned to Colonel William Malcolm's regiment known as the Malcolms. Easygoing Colonel Malcolm, who had neither talent nor interest in military matters, turned over his regiment to Burr. The Malcolms were in sad shape. Always the perfectionist, Burr set to work with the regiment the same way another perfectionist, Alexander Hamilton, had shaped up his company. Burr came down hard on discipline and drilling, but he also paid for extras out of his own pocket. Even though Major Burr looked like a teenager, he earned the Malcolms' respect and loyalty. A Malcolm officer later reported that the regiment was "a model for the whole army in discipline and order."

The Malcolms' duty was to protect the citizens from the British along the Ramapo Mountain Range in New York and New Jersey. In September 1777, when threatened by a large party of Redcoats, Burr led his Malcolms in an attack on a British outpost. Alarmed by all the farmers and militia who showed up to fight, the British pulled back. The local people recognized Burr as a hero, though Washington, as usual, did not.

While stationed in New Jersey, Burr met the charming and intellectual Theodosia Prevost. Although she came from a long line of loyal Americans, she was married to a British officer serving in the Caribbean. Burr was immediately attracted to Mrs. Prevost, and she to him.

Late that fall of 1777, Burr marched his Malcolms to Valley Forge, Pennsylvania, to spend the winter with Washington's main army. Because he'd earned a reputation for shaping up troops, Burr was put in charge of a rowdy militia unit guarding Gulph Pass, east of Valley Forge. Right away, he cracked down with drills, strict discipline, and surprise nighttime inspections.

But the militiamen weren't loyal Malcolms, and they resented this boyish-looking Colonel Burr who didn't give an inch. The story has been told that rumors of murdering him circulated. When Burr heard the rumors, he called for a night parade—but only after making sure cartridges were removed from all the guns.

Passing down the line of men, Burr came face-to-face with the ringleader. "Now is the time, my boys!" the ringleader shouted, and he pulled his trigger with a harmless click. At the same moment, Burr raised his sword and almost severed the man's arm. All talk of mutiny instantly ended.

After a freezing and starving winter at Valley Forge, Burr was happy to be reunited with his well-trained Malcolms. In June of 1778, he and his

Malcolms joined Washington's forces in hot pursuit of the British. With the temperature hovering at one hundred degrees, the two forces met at Monmouth Courthouse, New Jersey. During the battle, Burr and his Malcolms chased a party of Redcoats. Just as they were about to attack the British soldiers, Washington sent an order for them to hold back.

But that left Burr and his Malcolms in a dangerous position. Burr's horse was shot out from under him, and his second in command was killed. Surviving a day of death and brutal heat with his men, Burr suffered from devastating headaches and nausea. Sick or not, Burr, who believed the battle could have been won, was furious at Washington for allowing it to end in a draw.

After the Monmouth Courthouse battle, Colonel Burr's health didn't improve. In the fall, he wrote to Washington requesting a leave of absence for "a few months retirement and attention to my health." With the leave granted, Burr spent the next months with family and friends—and the enchanting Mrs. Prevost.

When Burr returned to duty, Washington appointed him commander of the Westchester Lines in New York State, which put him out of the action. At his "granny post," as the soldiers called it, he was ordered to prevent both British and American forces from stealing and looting.

But Burr couldn't handle even "granny" duty. Sick and weak, he resigned from the army. "I find my health unequal to the undertaking," he wrote to Washington in March 1779. Despite Burr's impressive military record, Washington undoubtedly had few regrets at seeing the last of *that* disrespectful young officer.

Retired or not, Burr had one more command. By chance, he was in New Haven, Connecticut, when it was reported that British troops were advancing toward New Haven. Quickly putting together a makeshift squad of local militia and Yale College students, Burr, with his hodge-podge force, held back the British long enough for the women and children of New Haven to escape. Once again, Burr was a hero to the local townspeople.

Although Burr was well enough to visit Mrs. Prevost often, he spent the next year trying to build up his strength. It was an unhappy time. He loved a married woman, his health was poor, and his law studies were at a standstill.

For the past few years, Burr had been exchanging letters with "a particular friend," Robert Troup, whom he had met when they were both army officers in New York City. In the spring of 1780, Burr asked Troup to join him in studying for their law exams.

Troup was enthusiastic. "My happiness, and my improvement in the law, depend entirely upon pursuing my studies with you."

Over the next year, Burr and Troup, who had been Alexander Hamilton's college roommate, studied law together, with Burr sometimes putting in a sixteen-hour day with his books, just as he had at the College of New Jersey.

Burr was twenty-five and hard at work studying law when he heard that Colonel Prevost had died. Although Theodosia Prevost had five children, was ten years older than Burr, and had cancer, which she called "my ill health," he loved her deeply. "She had the truest of hearts," he said, "the ripest of intellects, and the most winning and graceful manners of any woman."

Aaron Burr and Theodosia Prevost could now marry.

If Aaron Burr never claimed that he had rescued Captain Alexander Hamilton from the Bayard's Hill outpost when the British invaded Manhattan, neither did Hamilton. But Hamilton did claim that he had led a rearguard action. "I was among the last of our army that left the city," he boasted.

Commander in Chief Washington first noticed Hamilton when they were both at Harlem Heights. One of Hamilton's sons later wrote that Washington "invited him to his tent, and received an impression of his military talent."

While Aaron Burr was serving as General Putnam's aide in the fall of 1776, Hamilton was with Washington and three thousand soldiers fleeing across New Jersey in a ragged retreat after losing New York City to the British. At New Brunswick, Hamilton's artillery company brought up the rear and successfully held back the British with constant cannon fire so that the American troops could safely cross the Delaware River from New Jersey into Pennsylvania.

In December 1776, Hamilton and his artillery company again crossed the Delaware River with Washington, this time from Pennsylvania to New Jersey. Once in New Jersey, they marched to Trenton to wage a surprise attack on Christmas night, a victory that sent American morale sky-high.

Nine days later, Americans were again thrilled when Washington and his troops staged another successful surprise attack on the British, this time in Princeton, New Jersey. How did Hamilton feel about bombarding the college that had once rejected him? He never said.

Twenty-two-year-old Captain Hamilton was now being noticed. His disciplined artillery company was being noticed, too. "At their head was a boy . . . Hamilton of whom we had already heard so much," an officer said.

Washington already had his eye on Hamilton. He not only promoted Hamilton to colonel, but he also appointed him to his "family" as an aide-de-camp. Hamilton was flattered, but, like Burr, he wanted a battlefield command, not a desk job. While Burr was Washington's aide for only ten days, Hamilton stuck it out for four years.

Before long, Hamilton was Washington's chief secretary. "The pen for our army was held by Hamilton," Robert Troup said. Soon Washington was calling Hamilton "my boy," though in response, Washington was always "Your Excellency." And Washington's "family" took to Hamilton, too. One aide said Hamilton was "frank, affable, intelligent and brave." Because Hamilton could also be tough as nails, another aide tagged him "The Little Lion."

While Burr and his Malcolms were patrolling New Jersey in 1777, Hamilton was with Washington fighting the British in Pennsylvania—unsuccessfully. When the Americans lost the Battle of Brandywine, Washington ordered Hamilton to burn the flour mills along the Schuylkill River to prevent the British from capturing them.

As Hamilton and three soldiers were torching the mills, British dragoons charged. The four Americans jumped in a boat and pushed off. When a spray of gunfire killed one man, Hamilton and his companions dove into the water, swam to shore, and then hiked back to headquarters. They were greeted with open arms. They had been reported killed, but here they were, soaking wet but alive.

A week later, the British occupied the capital of Philadelphia.

At least Americans won big at Saratoga, New York, in October 1777. It was a victory that convinced the French to send ships and troops to America. Fluent in French, Hamilton translated, read, and wrote letters for all of Washington's French connections.

But when the army went into winter quarters at Valley Forge, Hamilton wasn't with them. He was so desperately sick with "fevers and violent rheumatic pain" that he almost died. Two months passed before he could make it to Valley Forge, no doubt arriving through Colonel Burr's Gulph Pass command post.

The following spring, the British abandoned Philadelphia and fled across New Jersey with Washington's troops hard on their heels. For the first time, Hamilton and Burr fought in the same battle, the battle of Monmouth Courthouse. Hamilton charged to the front in what one officer called "a frenzy of valor." But Hamilton's horse was shot out from under him, just as Burr's horse was killed in the same battle.

As the war fired up in the South and quieted down in the North, Hamilton spent the next year and a half doing here-and-there assignments for Washington. He delivered dispatches and orders, kept track of what the British were up to, and organized American troop and supply movements. On his own, he wrote letters to Congress offering his solution to the country's overwhelming money problems.

In December 1779, Hamilton traveled with Washington to Morristown, New Jersey, for the winter. The most pleasant part of winter headquarters was the dances, teas, and sleigh parties with local young women. If Hamilton and Burr shared one trait, it was their love for the ladies. And most of the ladies found the two charming young officers irresistible.

That winter, Elizabeth Schuyler arrived in Morristown. As soon as Hamilton met energetic, serious, dark-eyed Eliza, he fell in love. He had spent his youth flirting with young women, but now that he was in love, his flirting days were over. He told a friend that Eliza was "handsome . . . a belle . . . a saucy little charmer."

Hard as it was to leave Eliza, duty called him to West Point in New York State, where he met the fort's commander, General Benedict Arnold. The two men were waiting at Arnold's home for Washington to join them when a message was delivered. A British spy had just been captured. At the news, Arnold rushed from the room and didn't return, even after Washington had arrived. When Hamilton and another officer investigated, they found letters revealing that Arnold had plotted to sell West Point fortification plans to the British. A horrified Hamilton called it "the blackest treason."

Nevertheless, Hamilton sympathized with Arnold's hysterical wife, Peggy, who later fled to the home of her good friend, Theodosia Prevost. While at Mrs. Prevost's, Peggy confessed that she had talked her husband into turning traitor.

Hamilton fared better with the patriotic woman he loved. On December 14, 1780, he and Eliza Schuyler were married in the Schuylers' mansion in Albany, New York. Welcomed into the Schuyler clan, Hamilton must have felt a sense of family at last. And what a family it was, one of the wealthiest and most powerful in New York State.

The newlyweds joined Washington at his winter quarters in New

Windsor, New York. But relations had changed between the two men. Although Hamilton was desperate for a battle command, Washington still refused to give it to him. Two months later, Hamilton resigned from Washington's staff. This desk job had just gone on too long. "The great man and I have come to a rupture," was all Hamilton said.

At last, in 1781, while Burr and Robert Troup were deep into their law studies, Hamilton received command of an infantry battalion. By fall, he had joined sixteen thousand American and French troops laying siege to General Cornwallis's British forces at Yorktown, Virginia, for the final battle of the war.

"Fix bayonets!" Hamilton ordered on the night of October 14, 1781. "Follow me!"

At the head of three battalions, he dodged bullets in a quarter-of-a-mile dash across open ground to capture a British fortification. When the French seized the last outpost, the war was won.

A jubilant Hamilton wrote Eliza, "Tomorrow Cornwallis and his army are ours." And they were.

After five years, Hamilton returned home a hero for his courage in battle and for his service to his commander in chief. As a fourteen-year-old boy in St. Croix, Alexander Hamilton had dreamed of making a name for himself in war. That dream had come true, and then some.

Chapter 5

LAWYERS: 1781–1789

Aaron Burr knew that if he was going to marry Theodosia
Prevost, he'd better start earning some money. He'd have a wife to support *and* her children. But when he tried to get his New York law license in Albany, the capital of New York State, the judges turned him down. His one year of legal studies wasn't enough. He needed three.

That wouldn't do. Burr convinced the judges that war veterans like himself should receive special benefits. Almost before he knew it, Burr had his license. Aaron Burr and Theodosia Prevost were married in New Jersey on July 2, 1782. They set right off for Albany, New York.

Albany was still a frontier town with unpaved streets and only three thousand people. Frontier town or not, Burr planned to make both money and a name for himself. After all, he liked fine wines, fancy carriages, and expensive clothes; in other words, he liked to live well. But for now, there was a little problem of a "want of money," as Theo called their lack of funds. At least Burr's impressive family background swung open the gates to Albany society.

The Alexander Hamiltons were living in Albany, too, and Albany society had already welcomed them warmly. After all, Eliza Hamilton was a Schuyler, and the Schuylers ruled Albany. Burr and Hamilton had probably already met at some point, but as new young lawyers, they now struck up a friendship.

Life was good for the Burrs, and it got better with the birth of a girl, Theodosia, in 1783. Her mother pronounced her baby "a lovely daughter!"

But New York City beckoned.

As soon as the Revolutionary War officially ended in 1783, the British evacuated New York. Although Burr could picture caseloads of legal work just waiting for him in the city, a move to New York would cost more than he was "able to command." But with dependable Uncle Timothy Edwards coming through with a loan, the Burrs picked up and moved to New York.

The British had left the city in chaos. Almost two thousand buildings had been burned. Cows roamed garbage-filled streets. Buildings and churches had been used as hospitals, prisons, and storage dumps. The East Side was a run-down slum of tents and shacks.

Burr had guessed right. The chaos gave lawyers plenty of work, and he opened his own law office. Alexander Hamilton moved to New York, too, and, like Burr, opened a law office. Right away, both men felt at home in the fast-paced city, and two instant, loyal New Yorkers were born.

Burr and Hamilton, who both starred as trial lawyers, often tried the same cases, sometimes together, but mostly in opposition. But the courtroom stage brought out totally different performances. Burr was low-key, brief, and cool. Not Hamilton. He was fiery, argumentative, and talkative.

"Burr would say as much in half an hour as Hamilton in two hours," one judge said. A fellow lawyer analyzed their styles: "Hamilton addressed himself to the head only." Burr "first enslaved the heart and then led captive the head."

Still, the two men had a lot in common. Though Burr never forgot his family history, and Hamilton was haunted by his illegitimate birth, they were both brilliant and ambitious. And both insisted on being addressed by their military rank of Colonel. Because they lived in high style, they were often in debt, especially wildly extravagant Aaron Burr.

Burr had counted on making a name for himself in New York City, and he did. After only a year in New York, he was named to the New York State Assembly. But low-key as always, he almost never spoke up—until a bill was introduced to gradually end slavery. He jumped into the fray to argue that "gradually" wasn't good enough. The bill should abolish slavery at one fell swoop. The Assembly rejected both Burr's proposal and the bill.

Though Burr made noises about doing away with slavery, he owned household slaves for years. And even though Hamilton came on strong for abolishing slavery and was active in the New York Manumission Society, whose mission was to free the slaves, it was said that he owned one or two slaves himself, though that rumor was never proven.

Burr resigned from the Assembly after only a year. Overwhelmed by bills, he had to get back to earning serious money. To top off his income, he even took out-of-town cases, though he didn't much like traveling "from sloop to wagon, from wagon to canoe, and from canoe to sloop again." But 1785 was a good year. The Burrs had a second daughter, Sally.

From the heights, the Burrs sank to the depths. Three years later, Burr wrote to his brother-in-law: "We have lost our youngest child, our Sally, a beautiful lovely Baby." Burr himself still suffered from the "sick head-aches" and "eye trouble" he'd first experienced at the Monmouth Court-house battle, while Theo was well one day and in excruciating pain from cancer the next.

Difficult as life was for the Burrs, the new United States was taking great strides forward. In 1788, the Constitution became the supreme law of the land. George Washington was elected the nation's first president, with John Adams as his vice president. The Federalist party was the only political party in the country until a second political party began to form, the Democratic-Republican party.

By 1789, Burr had built an excellent reputation as a lawyer. That year, Democratic-Republican governor George Clinton asked him to become the State's attorney general in charge of New York State's legal matters. Burr hesitated. He called himself a "grave, secret sort of person," and he was. Even his friends said he was furtive and mysterious. Ever reluctant to commit himself, Burr had never come out as either a Democratic-Republican or a Federalist. But now that he'd had a taste of politics in the New York Assembly, he decided he liked the flavor.

Burr accepted Governor Clinton's offer. He may not have wanted to commit himself, but by becoming the attorney general of a Democratic-Republican governor, Aaron Burr put himself squarely in the Democratic-Republican camp.

As soon as Alexander Hamilton came back from the war in 1781, he began studying law. Pleasant as it was to live on the Schuylers' huge Albany estate, Alexander and Eliza Hamilton wanted a home of their own, and that took money. Good old Robert Troup from King's College days had studied law with Aaron Burr. Now he volunteered to tutor Hamilton so that Hamilton could earn his law license and start making money.

Thanks to Aaron Burr, war veterans no longer needed to study law for three years. Less than a year into his studies, war veteran Hamilton celebrated receiving his New York law license. And he celebrated the birth of his first child, Philip, in January, 1782. "Mrs. Hamilton has given me a fine boy," he crowed to a friend.

That he was both a war hero and the son-in-law of the powerful and wealthy Philip Schuyler didn't hurt Hamilton one bit. His Albany law practice thrived, and he and Eliza had a busy social life. And then, like Burr, he felt the pull of New York City.

The Hamiltons moved to New York all right, but their 57 Wall Street neighborhood wasn't as upscale as the Burrs' tonier 3 Wall Street address. Before long, the Hamiltons had two more children: a daughter, Angelica, and another son, Alexander. The Hamiltons even took in a young orphan.

Maybe Hamilton's sad childhood made him a loving father to his "darling little ones." One of his sons later wrote: "His gentle nature rendered his house a most joyous one to his children."

Much as Hamilton needed money to support his growing family, he took on needy clients who paid him with such fees as a barrel of ham or a flock of chickens. And because he believed all citizens had equal rights, he accepted clients who had been loyal to the British during the war. But New Yorkers who had suffered under the British occupation weren't happy about that.

Because both men possessed the ability to hypnotize juries, watching Hamilton and Burr argue a case in court soon became a New York sightseeing event. Hamilton's azure blue eyes, ruddy complexion, and reddish-brown hair, which he had a barber style every day, added up to a good-looking man. Though some people thought Hamilton was stiff and vain, one judge described him as "amiable, generous, tender, and charitable."

Hamilton added even more hours to his workday in 1784 when he founded the first bank in New York State, the Bank of New York. Hamilton was sure that the bank would help New York businesses recover from the war, and it did. Plus, the bank went a long way in unscrambling the confusing number of local, state, and foreign coins that circulated in the city.

New York was doing well, but the country wasn't. Like little children, the thirteen states quarreled about everything—their borders, money, taxes, and trade. Hamilton worried that the non-united United States wouldn't survive. So, like Burr before him, he put his law practice on hold and became a member of the New York Assembly. It was the nation's problems, he said, that "drew me again reluctantly into public life."

But Assemblyman Hamilton hadn't counted on having to travel. First he was sent to Maryland as a delegate to a conference in Annapolis that had been called to recommend changes in the laws that governed the country. Hamilton took center stage. He did more than recommend changes. He argued for a national convention that would reform the laws. Always a dynamic speaker, he got what he wanted: plans were made for every state to send delegates to a Constitutional Convention the following year.

That meant Hamilton took to the road again in 1787, this time to Philadelphia as a delegate to the Constitutional Convention. To Hamilton's delight, instead of talking about reforming the old laws, the delegates started right in talking about a whole new set of laws. Hamilton was known for never hesitating to voice his strong opinions. What a surprise that he said almost nothing at the convention!

Hamilton didn't agree with all the convention decisions, but at the end of that hot, steamy Philadelphia summer, on September 17, 1787, he and most of the other delegates signed the brand-new Constitution of the United States of America. Their signatures, however, didn't make the Constitution a done deal. To become official, the Constitution had to be ratified, or approved, by nine of the thirteen states.

Now *that* was right down Hamilton's alley. He'd get New York to ratify the Constitution or know the reason why. And he wasn't bothered one bit that New York's most powerful politician, Governor George Clinton, opposed the Constitution. Right away, Hamilton fired off a newspaper article stating that Clinton had a "greater attachment to his *own power* than to the *public good.*" Clinton's cronies weren't going to put up with that insult. They retorted that Hamilton was "superficial" and "self-conceited."

Hamilton and Clinton were political enemies for the rest of their lives.

Hamilton next asked lawyers James Madison and John Jay to help him write essays defending the Constitution against every argument that could be raised against it. A New York newspaper published the eighty-five essays, titled *The Federalist*, later known as *The Federalist Papers*.

John Jay wrote five essays. James Madison did better with twenty-nine. A brilliant wordsmith, Hamilton ended up writing fifty-one. He wrote under such pressure that the printer often waited outside his office for an essay that he was still working on. When the essays were later printed as a six-hundred-page book, Thomas Jefferson called it "the best commentary on the principles of government which ever was written." If it wasn't the best, it came close to it. *The Federalist* has survived the test of time.

When the New York convention met to vote *yea* or *nay* on the Constitution, Governor Clinton fought tooth and nail to defeat it, while Hamilton gave his all, with twenty-six speeches in support of it. In the end, the Constitution squeaked through with a *yea*. Hamilton received all the credit, and rightfully so.

New York City celebrated by painting the town red with banners, floats, and a grand parade. Five thousand working men marched down Broadway raising the tools of their trade. Robert Troup had the honor of holding up a copy of the Constitution as he marched with other New York lawyers.

But the crowds cheered loudest for a huge float pulled by ten horses that was a replica of a ship called the *Hamilton*. One bystander was especially proud: Nicholas Cruger, Hamilton's former boss from St. Croix. Cruger had recognized young Alex's promise sixteen years before and had helped pave his way to America. Look at how that promise had been fulfilled!

Did Aaron Burr march with his fellow lawyers? Because he was out of town on business that summer, probably not. It didn't matter. He was sure to hear that Alexander Hamilton was the hero of the day.

Chapter 6

POLITICIANS: 1789–1797

Alexander Hamilton was riding high. Soon after George Washington became president in 1789, he asked Hamilton to be his secretary of the treasury. Though the salary of $3,500 a year wasn't much for a man with a wife and four children, Hamilton jumped at the chance to be chief money man and tax collector. Hadn't he been planning on how to solve the country's financial problems for years? It was, he boasted, a "situation in which I can do most good."

Problems certainly weren't in short supply. The United States had borrowed almost eighty million dollars from different countries and sources to wage the Revolutionary War. Now those millions had to be paid back. But Hamilton didn't panic. Somehow he'd raise the money. After all, winning the war had been worth the cost, hadn't it? "The debt of the United States," he pointed out, "was the price of liberty."

Still, Hamilton knew other countries wouldn't trust the United States until the money was repaid. He asked Congress to pass a bill that would combine all the states' and the federal government's debts into one lump sum for the federal government to pay. But southern congressmen voted against the bill. Since the South had pretty much repaid their debts, why should southerners contribute to paying off the debts of other states?

With brainpower needed to find a solution, three of the country's top brains—Secretary of the Treasury Alexander Hamilton, Secretary of State Thomas Jefferson, and Congressman James Madison—met for a dinner that changed history. During the evening, they came up with a plan to win over the southern congressmen. How about building the nation's capital in the South between Maryland and Virginia and calling it Washington? For the ten years that it would take to build Washington, Philadelphia would be the temporary capital. When the city of Washington was finished in 1800, the government would move to the new capital lock, stock, and barrel.

The southern congressmen were so pleased to have the country's capital in the South, they passed the bill. Huzza!

But having the temporary capital in Philadelphia for the next ten years ended New York City's five-year reign as the country's capital. Now Hamilton would have to find a house in Philadelphia where his family could live. He wanted one "as near my destined office as possible . . . as to the rent, the lower the better." He ended up renting a house so close to his office that he could almost roll out of bed and be at his desk.

Much as the Hamiltons hated to leave their beloved New York, they packed up and moved to Philadelphia in 1790. As the country's largest city and busiest seaport, Philadelphia was known as "the first town in

America." Although Philadelphians were both educated and enthusiastic about art, literature, and the theater, their city just didn't have New York's business energy or its exciting mix of nationalities, including Dutch, Swedes, Spaniards, Germans, English, French, and more.

Hamilton's first order of business was to get money into the empty government treasury. He knew that customs duties, or taxes, which were charged on everything coming into the country from abroad, brought in the most money, so right away he created a Customs Service. He had lighthouses, beacons, and buoys built; hired workers to maintain piers; and ordered construction of ten ships to patrol for smugglers. His infant fleet later became the United States Coast Guard.

Banks were never far from Hamilton's mind. His Bank of New York was a success. Why not open a national bank? No, Secretary of State Thomas Jefferson protested. The Constitution didn't permit a national bank. Hamilton argued that anything that wasn't forbidden by the Constitution was permitted, and the Constitution didn't forbid a national bank.

When President Washington read Hamilton's arguments, he agreed, and Hamilton's dream became a reality—the Bank of the United States. More importantly, Hamilton had proven once and for all that the Constitution was a flexible document that could adapt to changing conditions and circumstances.

Now that the national bank was issuing uniform paper money, why not mint uniform coins and get rid of all of the unmatched coins that were circulating? Yes! With that, Hamilton oversaw the founding of the U.S. Mint to produce federal dollars, ten-cent pieces, half-cent pieces, copper pennies, and half pennies.

Hamilton was so dynamic and creative that a circle of loyal supporters, called "gladiators," gathered around him. But not everyone was a fan. "Congress may go home. Mr. Hamilton is all-powerful, and fails in nothing he attempts," one senator grumbled.

Hamilton was far too busy to keep up with New York politics. So he was stunned when he heard that Aaron Burr was running for the United States Senate from New York. What was especially annoying was that Burr was running against Hamilton's father-in-law, Federalist Senator Philip Schuyler, whose Senate term was almost up. Hamilton immediately started writing letters and using his influence to defeat candidate Burr.

But Democratic-Republican Burr, backed by Governor George Clinton and New York's powerful Livingston family, won the election. A Federalist like his father-in-law, Hamilton was furious. He stormed that Burr was "one of the worst sort—a friend to nothing but as it suits his interest and ambition." Hamilton now looked on Burr as more than a courtroom rival—Burr was now a political foe.

Another political foe was the Democratic-Republican secretary of state, Thomas Jefferson. Federalist Hamilton called Jefferson a "man of profound ambition and violent passions," though Hamilton himself was both ambitious *and* hot-headed.

"As politicians," Jefferson remarked, "it was impossible for two men to be of more opposite principles." It was true.

Alexander Hamilton, as a Federalist, advocated both a strong central government and a strong presidency. He also believed that well-educated persons of means serving in office provided a stable force in the government.

On the other hand, as a Democratic-Republican, Thomas Jefferson favored a weak central government that would allow all classes of citizens to hold office, as well as govern themselves with little or no government interference.

Hamilton and Jefferson's public quarrels made President Washington very unhappy indeed, especially since each man was working behind the scenes to get the other to resign. Hamilton won that battle when Jefferson resigned in 1793.

But all politics took a backseat to a killer yellow-fever epidemic during that summer of 1793. Within months, four thousand Philadelphians had died. In September, Hamilton collapsed. His wife, Eliza, fell sick a few days later. In a lucky coincidence, Ned Stevens, Hamilton's "eternal friend" from his St. Croix childhood, lived in Philadelphia. Even better, as a doctor, Stevens had treated hundreds of yellow-fever victims in St. Croix. Instead of following the usual treatment of bleeding patients and making them vomit, he gave them quinine, tonics, and cold baths. He had both Hamiltons back on their feet in five days.

The following year, a different kind of trouble brewed. Pennsylvania farmers detested the new tax that Hamilton had slapped on liquor. Why wouldn't they? They grew grain that they distilled into whiskey. A senator predicted the tax would result in "war and bloodshed," and it did. In the Whiskey Rebellion that followed, farmers and distillers tarred and feathered tax collectors, stole their horses, and burned down their houses. The last straw came when five thousand rebels prepared to march on Philadelphia against the government.

President Washington called up the militia and put Hamilton in charge. Commanding troops was what Hamilton liked best, especially if he could win military honors. But when the farmers heard that Hamilton was headed their way with twelve thousand militiamen, their rebellion fizzled out without a shot being fired.

After serving for five years, Secretary of the Treasury Hamilton figured he'd done almost everything he had set out to do. Besides, with the birth of his fifth child, he could no longer make ends meet on his salary. In 1795, Hamilton resigned. "I am no longer a public man," he said. "I am once more a private person."

As "a public man," Alexander Hamilton had been a political giant, second in the country in power and influence to only President Washington. As "a private man," Hamilton returned with his family to New York City, where he resumed his law practice.

But bid farewell to politics? Never!

From 1789 to 1791, while Alexander Hamilton was serving as George Washington's secretary of the treasury, Aaron Burr was putting in two years as New York State attorney general facing a desk full of problems. Revolutionary War soldiers demanded their back pay, home owners sued for damages by the British, lenders demanded to be paid. Complaints were endless.

Two years as attorney general were enough for Burr. Besides, he was as ambitious as ever, and being attorney general was a political dead end. In 1791, he jumped on the national stage to run for the Senate from New

York against Alexander Hamilton's father-in-law, Philip Schuyler. Federalist Schuyler was head of one of New York's most powerful families, but the other two powerful New York families, the George Clintons and the Robert Livingstons, were Democratic-Republicans. With their support, Democratic-Republican Burr won hands down.

Always secretive, Burr almost never put anything important on paper, or if he did, he used a code. He once said, "Things written remain." But as the new senator from New York, thirty-five-year-old Burr couldn't resist bragging. "My election will be displeasing to several persons in Philadelphia," he wrote.

What an understatement! Back in the temporary capital of Philadelphia, Hamilton wasn't just displeased, he was seething. And instead of giving Burr credit for winning, he accused Burr of backroom high jinks.

No longer dipping his toe in the political waters, Burr was now diving in headfirst. He had once been undecided about a career. Now he'd found a lifelong love—politics—which he called "a great deal of fun." And just as Hamilton had his gladiators, Burr was soon surrounded by loyal supporters called "Burrites."

With Senate sessions held in Philadelphia, Burr arrived a week early to look for a house. Hamilton hadn't found house hunting easy, and neither did Burr. He wrote his wife, Theo, that he was "having some trouble . . . because I am difficult to please . . . good accomodations are hard to find." And being short of money made it harder. Burr would be earning only six dollars a day.

Although Burr moved to Philadelphia, his heart was not only still in New York politics, but it was also with Theo, who disliked the capital and refused to live there. Furthermore, her cancer had progressed, and she was often bedridden. Burr, however, was more than ambitious, he was also clever. He decided he could kill two birds with one stone and return to New York with honor. He would run for governor of New York. But after less than a year in the Senate, he received so little support that he shelved his dream . . . for the time being.

Burr soon had another dream. Why not put his name up as the Democratic-Republican candidate for vice president in the 1792 election? "He is for or against nothing but as it suits his interest or ambition," Hamilton snapped when he heard Burr's plans. "I feel it is my religious duty to oppose his career."

Hamilton didn't have to work very hard. Despite Burr's efforts, the Democratic-Republicans nominated George Clinton to run with Thomas Jefferson. But Jefferson and Clinton didn't get anywhere, either. President Washington and Vice President John Adams, both Federalists, won a second term.

And then in 1794, the year that George Washington appointed Hamilton to be in charge of putting down the Whiskey Rebellion, Theodosia Burr died. Burr described his wife as "the woman who brought me more happiness than all my success." Devastated by her death, he no longer felt an urgent need to return to New York. For the time being, he would play at being a senator.

But with his political future now his main concern, Burr didn't like to commit himself on Senate votes until he knew which way most of the senators planned to vote. And because he didn't always vote with the other Democratic-Republicans, they didn't trust him as "one of them," as one senator expressed it.

Although Burr may have hesitated to commit himself on most of the Senate votes, he didn't hesitate to oppose most, if not all, of Washington and Hamilton's programs. In 1794, Burr voted against Washington's appointment of John Jay as special minister to Great Britain. And when John Jay came back from Great Britain with a treaty to ease rising tensions between the two countries, Burr opposed the Jay Treaty as well.

Senator Burr may have schemed against Washington, but Washington also schemed against Burr. When Burr started doing research at the State Department to write a history of the Revolutionary War, Washington ordered him to stop snooping in State Department files. Furious, Burr considered the order as a personal insult from his old commander in chief. (It probably was.)

Washington snubbed Burr once again when he was considering whom to appoint as the new minister to France. Burr wanted the post. But when Burr's name was submitted, Washington replied that he never appointed any person he believed was lacking integrity. Supporters submitted Burr's name again. A second no. And when they arrived with Burr's name for the third time, Washington refused to see them. Right or wrong, Burr always blamed Hamilton for turning Washington against him.

Angry as Burr was at not getting the French minister's post, he once again tried to drum up interest in a run for New York governor in the 1795 election. But the media wasn't about to jump on the Burr bandwagon. One reporter came down on Burr "not because I know him to belong to either one faction or another, but because I believe him to belong to none."

Horrified that Burr might become governor of New York, Hamilton did his best to block him. And his best succeeded. He convinced the first chief justice of the Supreme Court, John Jay, to run as the Federalist candidate for governor. Popular John Jay won the governorship easily.

Burr raged that, at every step he tried to take, Hamilton blocked his way.

But resolute as always, Senator Burr didn't give up. The very next year, he found bigger fish to fry: the vice presidency of the United States. No politician was more of a self-promoter than Burr, and he became "industrious" in writing letters and contacting everyone he knew to support him in the 1796 election. The Democratic-Republicans, now known as Republicans, nominated Thomas Jefferson as candidate for president and Burr to run with him. Candidate Aaron Burr stirred up little enthusiasm.

Because the Constitution called for the candidate with the most electoral votes to become president, and the candidate with the second highest number of votes to serve as vice president, a badly matched twosome was elected. Federalist John Adams was elected president, and Republican Thomas Jefferson vice president. Devastated to receive the fewest number of votes, Burr's spirits weren't helped when a Virginia politician remarked: "I have watched the movements of Mr. Burr with attention, and have discovered traits of character which sooner or later will give us much trouble."

Burr's six-year Senate term was up the following year. Having lost every election but his 1791 Senate race, like it or not, Burr had no choice but to go back to New York and pick up his law practice where he'd left off. At least he could live in the city he loved.

Everyone assumed that Burr was finished in politics. But they didn't know how resolute he could be. Like Alexander Hamilton, Aaron Burr may have gone back to the law, but he had no intention whatsoever of being done with politics.

Chapter 7

FRIENDS: 1797–1800

When President Washington retired in 1797, all of Alexander Hamilton's ties with the White House were cut off. Why wouldn't they be? Even as a New York lawyer no longer in political office, Hamilton was the country's leading Federalist, and he had bypassed Federalist John Adams in the 1796 presidential election to support another Federalist candidate. Adams was elected president, but he was enraged at Hamilton's lack of support and never forgave him.

But Hamilton soon had a bigger problem on his hands than Adams. James Callender, a sleazy newspaper reporter, wrote that Hamilton was guilty of dishonest dealings with government funds when he was secretary of the treasury. Proof? He was paying blackmail to a man named James Reynolds.

That was an outrageous accusation! Hamilton immediately published a pamphlet giving his side of the story. Yes, he was paying Reynolds blackmail, he admitted, but not for cheating the government. He was paying Reynolds to keep quiet about a romance that he'd had with Reynolds's wife, Maria. "My real crime is an amorous connection with his wife," Hamilton confessed.

What was called the Reynolds pamphlet created an instant uproar. Hamilton's friends were stunned. One "gladiator" called the pamphlet "humiliating in the extreme." Though Hamilton loved his wife and children, apparently he would rather betray his family than be branded as a crook dipping into the government treasury.

The confession gave the Republicans the perfect opportunity to clobber Hamilton in the newspapers. And they did. Surprisingly, Aaron Burr was more understanding than his Republican buddies. He said he hadn't doubted Hamilton's integrity as secretary of the treasury and he didn't doubt his integrity now.

About all that distracted the public from the Reynolds pamphlet was news that French privateers were seizing American ships at sea. Relieved to move on, Hamilton approved of President Adams's decision to send envoys to France for peace talks. And he approved of Adams's decision to enlarge the navy. "Real firmness is good for everything. Strut is good for nothing," Hamilton declared.

But the peace talks failed, and tensions with the French increased. In 1798, President Adams asked George Washington to head up a provisional army. Washington was willing to serve *if* Hamilton was appointed his second in command with the rank of inspector general. Much as he disliked Hamilton, Adams agreed. Hamilton, who had craved military glory since he was fourteen, was delighted.

The Quasi War, or not-quite-real war, with France became deadly serious. And now that he had a military commission, Hamilton no longer wanted peace. After all, as second in command, General Hamilton could make a name for himself if war broke out.

When Aaron Burr returned to New York City after his Senate term was up, Hamilton was cordial to him, mostly because Burr hinted that he might switch from the Republican party to the Federalist party. "Little Burr! I fancy he now begins to think he was wrong and I was right," Federalist Hamilton boasted. He even recruited Burr to work with him on fortifying New York's harbors against a possible French attack.

Always a workaholic, General Hamilton let his law practice slide as he put all of his efforts into preparing for war. "Hamilton's hobby was the army," Adams mocked. And it was. With his usual gusto, Hamilton organized the troops, stocked ammunition, ordered supplies, wrote training books, and designed uniforms—including his own elegant uniform.

And then the French began to back down. They would meet for peace talks after all. When President Adams appointed peace envoys, Hamilton was furious. To talk Adams out of making such a foolish move, Hamilton confronted him face-to-face. Adams called the meeting "unforeseen, unrequested, and undesired . . . a sample of his habitual impudence." With near hysteria, Hamilton didn't get anywhere changing John Adams's mind. Their meeting was so hostile that the two men never spoke to each other again.

Even though peace was a possibility, General Hamilton continued to work full-time on army preparations. And then, out of the blue, Aaron Burr gave him a chance to help his fellow New Yorkers.

Polluted wells were fingered as the culprit when a yellow-fever epidemic struck New York in 1798. Burr told Hamilton that he wanted to create a water company called the Manhattan Company to pipe pure water from the Bronx River into the city. Would Hamilton help him? Hamilton most certainly would. Using all of his skills as a lawyer, Hamilton was the key figure in seeing to it that the New York Assembly passed approval of the Manhattan Company.

But the creation of the Manhattan Company and the birth of a seventh child were about Hamilton's only high moments in 1799. With so much effort spent on the army, his law practice was floundering, and he was short of cash. In June, Hamilton heard that his father had died on a small Caribbean island. Although he hadn't seen his father since he was eleven, the news was unsettling. Only a few months later, he was dismayed to hear that the peace envoys had sailed for France. And then, as an unhappy ending to an unhappy year, George Washington, Hamilton's mentor and friend since 1776, died in December. "My imagination is gloomy, my heart sad," Hamilton mourned.

Finally, in 1800, a peace treaty with France ended the Quasi War. Peace ended any need for the provisional army, dashing Hamilton's hopes for military glory. Still angry at Adams for his successful peace efforts, Hamilton became obsessed that year with defeating Adams in his run for a second term as president. Hamilton's battle cry? "Adams is out of the question."

Republicans nominated Thomas Jefferson for president and Aaron Burr, of all people, to also run. Because Hamilton certainly didn't want to see Adams reelected, and he didn't want to see Jefferson or Burr in the White House, either, he supported Federalist Charles Pinckney for president.

For the time being, Federalist Hamilton zeroed in on Federalist Adams with a pamphlet that was as shocking as the Reynolds pamphlet. In his pamphlet, he accused Adams of being unbalanced, with a "disgusting egotism . . . vanity without bounds . . . outrageous behavior . . . ungovernable temper."

The Federalists were livid. Was Hamilton trying to destroy his own party? Sure enough, Hamilton's Adams pamphlet, along with Federalist anger at the peace mission, defeated John Adams, even though Adams's peace efforts had saved the United States from what might have been a disastrous war with France.

Republicans Thomas Jefferson and Aaron Burr won the election. But to Hamilton's astonishment, *and* the country's, Jefferson and Burr tied for president.

No wonder December of 1800 found Hamilton more depressed than ever. He was still dealing with the old Reynolds scandal. With his law practice limping along, he had serious money problems. He had lost all clout with the Federalist party. The peace treaty had cost him his chance for military fame. Worst of all, either Thomas Jefferson or Aaron Burr would become the next president, and it might be months before the dilemma could be resolved.

"At the bottom of my soul," Alexander Hamilton confessed to Eliza, "there is a more than usual gloom."

In 1797, Aaron Burr finished up his six-year Senate term
and returned to New York City, which had now been lawyer Hamilton's
home base for two years. Burr was finally home, too, but he missed having
his beloved Theo there to greet him. At least his lovely fourteen-year-old
daughter, Theodosia, welcomed her papa home.

Theodosia was a bright young woman, and Burr had always believed
that girls should have the same education as boys. Hadn't his wife proved
how intellectually gifted women could be? In what he called a "fair experi-
ment," Burr put Theodosia on a tough schedule of French, Latin, Greek,
mathematics, literature, geography, spelling, dancing, piano, the harp, and
riding. "Your translation of the comedy into French, if not finished, must
go on," he scolded. "Some English or French history must employ a little
of every day."

When she was seventeen, Theodosia's schooling ended. How proud her
papa was! "Many are surprised that I could repose in you so great a trust;
but I knew that you were equal to it," Burr applauded.

Soon after he returned to New York, Burr was as stunned as everyone
else by Hamilton's confession that he was being blackmailed for a secret
romance with Maria Reynolds. Although Burr had recently been squiring

women around, he had always been careful to keep his private life private. Although he no doubt thought Hamilton was out of his mind to confess to a romantic intrigue, he publicly vouched for Hamilton's honor as the country's secretary of the treasury.

Burr did more than speak out. He also may have saved Hamilton's life once again. Hamilton was convinced that it was former Republican senator and future president of the United States James Monroe who had leaked the blackmail story to the press, and he angrily accused him. Monroe wouldn't admit to it or apologize. As a gentleman, Hamilton, whose honor had been questioned, challenged Monroe, also a gentleman, to a duel. Although a duel seemed inevitable, Aaron Burr, whom Monroe had asked to support him as his second, took on the role of peacemaker. Thanks to Burr's masterly art of persuasion, the duel never happened.

And then, as war preparations with France built up, Alexander Hamilton stepped forward for Burr. Like Hamilton, Burr was drawn to the military. With a nudge from Burr, General Hamilton asked Washington to commission Burr as a brigadier general in the provisional army, with the hope that "the Administration may manifest a cordiality to him." Absolutely not! Washington had never trusted Burr, and he didn't trust him now.

Was there no end to Washington humiliating him? Burr let off steam to John Adams. He raged that he "despised Washington as a Man of No Talents, and one who could not spell a sentence of common English."

So, instead of serving in the army, Burr worked with Hamilton on a military committee to strengthen New York's harbors. The two men were so cordial that Robert Troup, a friend to both, was astonished. He could hardly believe that he had seen Aaron and Alexander talking to each other in a friendly way.

Hamilton stepped in again to ask Governor John Jay if he would appoint Burr superintendent of the New York harbor fortifications. "Col. Burr will be very equal to it and will I believe undertake it," Hamilton wrote to Jay.

Perhaps Jay remembered that, years ago, Senator Burr had voted against his appointment as special minister to Great Britain, as well as voting against the Jay Treaty, which was designed to ease tensions with Great Britain. Whatever the reason, Jay never replied to Hamilton's request.

Having failed at getting a military commission and the harbor super-intendent's position, Burr was back to politics. He ran for the Assembly in the New York legislature and won. Burr's friends thought that such a lowly position was far beneath a former U.S. senator. Robert Troup even told Burr that being a member of the New York Assembly was "beneath his talents."

But always resolute, Burr was looking ahead. He planned to use his seat in the Assembly as a base from which to launch his campaign for presi-dent in the 1800 election. As soon as Burr was sworn into the Assembly, he began working on eight or ten key Federalists to convince them to switch to the Republican party.

Burr also used his Assembly seat in other, not so legal, ways. He arranged for a Dutch company to pay several Assembly members, including himself, to vote for bills that would benefit the company. The company also hinted broadly that it would pay the assemblymen for special favors.

John Church, Hamilton's brother-in-law, got wind of the deal and accused Burr of bribery. With his honor at stake, Burr challenged Church to a duel. When the two men dueled, Church's bullet struck Burr's jacket, while Burr missed Church entirely. With that, the duel ended and everyone went home.

Years before, Burr had acquired the Richmond Hill mansion that he had first seen when it was Washington's New York headquarters during the war. But maintaining and furnishing the mansion was a drain on Burr's pocketbook, and he was heavily in debt. As a Republican, Burr had no luck borrowing money from New York's only two banks, both founded by Federalist Alexander Hamilton: the Bank of New York and the New York branch of the Bank of the United States.

Burr made up his mind. What New York needed was a bank that was friendly to Republicans, like himself.

The yellow-fever epidemic of 1798 gave Burr his opportunity. He proposed a bill to the Assembly that would create the Manhattan Company to pipe "pure and wholesome water" into New York City. Next Burr lined up New York's most respected men, including Alexander Hamilton, to help him get the bill passed in the Assembly. Of everyone on the committee, Hamilton worked the hardest to persuade assemblymen to vote approval of Burr's company.

But Burr's motives for establishing the Manhattan Company weren't as altruistic as they seemed. Burr's mother had called Aaron "sly." Washington called him an "intriguer." They were both right. Just before the bill was voted on, Burr added an "extra" that almost no one noticed. The "extra" gave the Manhattan Company permission to do whatever it wanted with leftover funds. In other words, the Manhattan Company could open a bank. The bill passed with ease.

Burr didn't waste any time. The Manhattan Bank, which later became the Chase Manhattan Bank, opened five months later. Although "pure and wholesome" water never flowed into New York City from the Bronx River, the Manhattan Company did sink a well and also pumped water from the Chambers Street reservoir that was distributed to a small section of the city through wooden pipes.

Because borrowing money from the new bank eased Burr's money problems, he was able to put all his energy into the upcoming Assembly election. Political campaigning had always been low-key, but now Republican Burr went to town. Unlike other politicians of the day, he organized a Republican committee to raise funds, appointed subcommittees, held open houses, convinced prominent Republicans to run for office, made speeches, and, last but not least, spied on what the Federalists were doing.

Burr's efforts paid off. Republicans won thirteen Assembly seats, which gave them the majority in the Assembly. The Republicans in the Assembly were then able to elect twelve Republican electors for the upcoming 1800 national election. These electors, each of whom cast two votes of equal weight for president and vice president, could be counted on to vote for the Republican candidates. Even before the election, Burr boasted to a Federalist, "We have beat you by superior *Management*."

The Republicans, however, didn't nominate Burr for president as he had hoped. Their man was Thomas Jefferson. But the Republicans did reward Burr for his hard work by nominating him to run with Jefferson.

When the voting closed, it was clear that Thomas Jefferson and Aaron Burr had defeated John Adams and Charles Pinckney. Robert Troup noted that Burr was "in very high glee." After all the votes were counted, Burr's glee shot up to another level. He and Jefferson had tied for president with seventy-three electoral votes each. Maybe, just maybe, he would become president after all.

Aaron Burr now faced a showdown. And so did the country.

Chapter 8

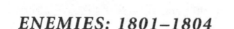

ENEMIES: 1801–1804

BURR

A tie between Aaron Burr and Thomas Jefferson for president! Now what? Now it was up to the Constitution, and the Constitution dictated that it was the responsibility of the House of Representatives to break the tie.

Aaron Burr had three choices. He could step out of the picture graciously and let Jefferson become president, which was what the Republicans wanted. Or he could try to convince members of the House of Representatives to vote for him. Or he could do nothing.

In the end, he did nothing. Instead, he returned to New York for his daughter's wedding. Theodosia was married to a wealthy southerner, Joseph Alston, in February 1801, just nine days before the House of Representatives was to meet to decide on the country's next president.

The Republicans in the House were determined to elect their leader, Thomas Jefferson. The Federalists in the House were stuck with having to make a choice between two Republicans. Most of the Federalists viewed Jefferson as an atheist with radical ideas, while Burr seemed "safe."

But "safe" wasn't a word that Federalist Alexander Hamilton would use to describe Burr. Despite Hamilton's dislike of Jefferson and memories of their bitter political battles, he believed Jefferson had more integrity and greater ability than Burr. With a barrage of negative letters to Federalists in the House of Representatives, Hamilton labeled Burr "the most unfit and dangerous man in the community."

Now that three new states had joined the Union, winning the presidency would take a majority vote of nine states out of the sixteen. Day after day, members of the House of Representatives voted. Day after day, neither Burr nor Jefferson won a majority. At last, enough representatives withdrew their support of Burr so that on the thirty-sixth ballot, Jefferson was elected president. As runner-up, Aaron Burr became his vice president.

Furious, Burr blamed Hamilton's anti-Burr letters for his defeat. On the other hand, doing nothing hadn't earned Burr the respect he had hoped for. "Had Burr done anything for himself he would long ere this have been president," one of the representatives pointed out.

And Burr's refusal to hand over the presidency voluntarily to Jefferson before the House began to vote cost him dearly. From then on, Burr was on Jefferson's blacklist, not a good list to be on. Jefferson destroyed Burr's political power in New York by seeing to it that George Clinton was elected governor. Next, he appointed the Republican Clintons and Livingstons to fill all of New York's political jobs. Vice President Burr was "completely an insulated man in Washington; wholly without personal influence," a reporter noted.

Burr found being odd man out hard enough without having to cope with life in the new capital. In 1801, Washington was a ramshackle village of boardinghouses, work sheds, piles of lumber and bricks, and half-finished buildings, including the White House and the Capitol. The constant din of construction was deafening. Stray cattle and pigs wandered the muddy streets.

Always on the lookout for a party or a lovely lady, Burr asked a fellow politician about Washington nightlife. "Evening amusement?" came the reply. "There is no such thing."

As vice president, Burr's only job was to act as president of the Senate. One senator, at least, praised him: "He always understands the subject before the Senate, states the question clearly, and confines the speakers to the point."

Allowed to vote only if there was a tie in the Senate, Burr hesitated to commit himself . . . as always. His unpredictable voting record irritated Republicans and Federalists alike.

During those difficult vice-presidential years, Burr's happiest times were when his daughter, Theodosia, and her family visited. He doted on his baby grandson, Aaron Burr Alston, who called him Gampy, and though Burr courted many women, his daughter remained his one true love.

In 1804, another presidential election loomed. To prevent future ties, Amendment XII to the Constitution was ratified. The amendment gave each elector the customary two votes, but the two votes would no longer be equal. Instead, one vote would be cast for president and the other vote for vice president.

Burr was realistic enough to know his vice presidential days would soon be over, and they were. Jefferson tapped New Yorker George Clinton to run as his vice president. Still as resolutely political as ever, Burr tossed his hat into the ring as a candidate for governor of New York, but this time as an Independent with no party ties. With the Republican Clintons and Livingstons ruling New York, he knew his best bet was to court the Federalists as well as pick up what unhappy Republican voters he could find.

Hamilton, who backed New York Supreme Court Justice Morgan Lewis for governor, once again picked up his pen against Burr. "Hamilton is intriguing for any candidate who can have a chance of success against AB [Aaron Burr]," Burr seethed in a letter to his daughter.

Sure enough, in the 1804 election, Morgan Lewis defeated Aaron Burr to become New York's governor. Burr was livid. He had been soundly rejected by both parties, and although he would be vice president for another eleven months, for all intents and purposes, his political life was over. Although he always seemed outwardly cool, Burr nursed a serious temper, and all of his rage was directed at Alexander Hamilton. He told a friend how Hamilton "had a peculiar habit of saying things improper and offensive." Just count the times that Hamilton had blocked, or tried to block, his ambitions. Five!

The first time was when Burr had run against Hamilton's father-in-law, Philip Schuyler, for senator in 1791, and Hamilton had pulled out all the stops to defeat him. He'd even called Burr "unprincipled, both as a public and private man." Burr looked back at winning that election as his most satisfying victory.

But soon after that, President Washington had refused to appoint him as minister to France. Burr was sure that as payback for defeating Hamilton's father-in-law, Hamilton had convinced Washington to reject Burr for the minister's post that he wanted so badly.

Only a few years later, in the election for governor of New York, Hamilton had guaranteed Burr's defeat when he talked John Jay, first chief justice of the Supreme Court, into becoming a candidate. Jay was just too popular, and too highly respected, for Burr to have any chance of winning.

The worst was when Hamilton cost Burr the presidency by urging Federalists in the House of Representatives to back Thomas Jefferson. True or not, Burr clung to the belief that Hamilton's influence was the reason he lost.

And now, with his glib pen, Hamilton had thwarted him again by destroying Burr's second chance to become governor of New York, as well as destroying Burr's last opportunity to make a political comeback.

As if his pen didn't do enough damage, at a private dinner party, Hamilton again called Burr "a dangerous man and one who ought not to be trusted." But Hamilton's comment didn't stay private for long. A guest at the party, Charles Cooper, repeated the remark in a letter that a New York newspaper picked up and printed. Cooper then wrote another letter describing "a still more despicable opinion which General Hamilton has expressed of Mr. Burr." Although Cooper didn't say what Hamilton's "despicable opinion" of Mr. Burr had been, a newspaper printed the second letter, too.

After years of conspiring behind his back, Hamilton had now insulted Burr up front and in print. "General Hamilton had at different times and upon various occasions used language and expressed opinions highly injurious to [my] reputation," Burr stormed. Heavily in debt, with no political power, Burr had only one thing left: his honor. His fury ignited into action, and he demanded that Hamilton tell him what the "despicable opinion" had been.

But Hamilton refused to explain anything. For five days, Burr and Hamilton exchanged increasingly chilly letters. Because mail was often opened, passed around, and published in newspapers, two men—William Van Ness, a longtime Burrite, and Nathaniel Pendleton, Hamilton's trusted friend—acted as messengers to hand deliver the letters.

Each letter cut off one more opportunity for the two men to come to an understanding. Both Van Ness and Pendleton urged Burr and Hamilton to patch up their differences, but neither man would give an inch. On June 27, Van Ness, who had now become Burr's second, delivered to Pendleton a formal challenge for a duel.

Hamilton accepted the challenge.

Date: July 11, 1804. Place: Weehawken, New Jersey.

During the two weeks before the duel, Burr spent a lot of time alone, brooding over his political misfortunes and his financial troubles. He considered selling his estate to pay his debts, but he loved Richmond Hill too much to take such a drastic step.

Without telling his daughter about the upcoming duel, Burr gave her instructions concerning his slaves. And he asked her to burn all his personal correspondence, especially his correspondence with women. In his last letter, he told her how much he loved her: "I am indebted to you, my dearest Theodosia, for a very great portion of the happiness which I have enjoyed in this life. You have completely satisfied all that my heart and affections had hoped or even wished."

The night before the duel, Aaron Burr fell asleep in his Richmond Hill library. He slept soundly and woke only when William Van Ness arrived to accompany him across the Hudson River to Weehawken.

Alexander Hamilton, like everyone else, was caught by surprise when Aaron Burr and Thomas Jefferson tied for president in the election of 1800. He had certainly had his political differences with Jefferson, but at least Jefferson had a vision for the country. The only vision Aaron Burr had was to gain power and money for himself. "In my opinion," Hamilton declared, "he is inferior in real ability to Jefferson." He warned Federalists that if they supported Burr for president, they would be "signing their own death warrant."

Although Hamilton did his best to defeat Burr, for the first time ever, he was in political limbo himself, and his depression deepened. In the end, to his relief, Thomas Jefferson was elected.

Gradually, as Hamilton began to turn more and more to religion, and spent longer stretches of time with his wife and seven children, his sense of failure lifted. And when he bought thirty-five acres of land in Harlem Heights that overlooked the Hudson River on one side and the Harlem and East Rivers on the other, he discovered a new source of joy. He had a handsome house built, which he named the Grange after his Scottish ancestor's estate. "'Tis here only I can find true pleasure," he wrote of his new home, which was only a half mile or so from Aaron Burr's Richmond Hill mansion.

Hamilton had hardly begun to furnish his new house when the family suffered a tragedy that would change their lives forever. The Hamiltons were proud of their oldest child, Philip. Hamilton, who described Philip as the family's "eldest and *brightest* hope," was sure that his brilliant and handsome son would achieve "future greatness."

But in November 1801, nineteen-year-old Philip exchanged ugly words with a young lawyer, George Eacker, who had attacked Alexander Hamilton in a speech. Though Philip demanded an apology, Eacker refused. Because neither Philip nor Eacker would back down, they agreed that only a duel would settle the matter.

Hamilton couldn't talk Philip out of the duel, but he could advise his son not to raise his pistol in the hope that Eacker wouldn't raise his. When the duel began, Philip did as his father advised and held his gun to his side. So did Eacker. The two young men stared silently at each other. Then Eacker raised his pistol. When Philip raised his, Eacker shot him.

Fatally wounded, Philip was carried to his uncle's home. Upon seeing his son, Hamilton cried out to his friend, Dr. David Hosack, "Doctor, I despair." And then he fainted. The grieving Hamilton family sat with Philip through the worst night of their lives. Philip died at five the next morning.

Hamilton couldn't be consoled. Robert Troup described his old friend's sorrow: "Never did I see a man so completely overwhelmed by grief as Hamilton has been." His face was "etched with grief." To add to the family's heartbreak, seventeen-year-old Angelica, who had adored her older brother, suffered a mental and emotional breakdown from which she never recovered.

The Hamiltons' only bright moment during that year was the birth of their eighth child not long after their oldest son's death. They named the baby Philip.

Although Hamilton never completely got over Philip's death, his interest in New York politics slowly began to revive. To his astonishment, in 1802, Republican Aaron Burr appeared at a Federalist meeting, where he offered a toast to a "union of all honest men." Burr an honest man? Hardly. Hamilton assumed that Burr had come to the meeting to win Federalist votes.

Hamilton was right. Burr announced he would run for governor of New York as an independent in the election of 1804. Hamilton didn't want Burr as New York's governor in 1804 any more than he had wanted Burr as governor in 1795.

But at this point in his career, Hamilton had little political influence. About all he could do was speak up on behalf of New York Supreme Court Justice Morgan Lewis for governor. But when Lewis won, an angry Burr and his friends blamed Hamilton. "If General Hamilton had not opposed Colonel Burr, I have very little doubt but he would have been governor of New York," a Burrite raged.

In turn, Hamilton was furious at Aaron Burr. And he was furious at himself. He had worked hard to make sure Burr's Manhattan Company was approved so that pure water from the Bronx River could flow into New York City. Knowing that Burr was sly and devious, he should have realized that the Manhattan Company was a fraud. Burr had just used the company as an excuse to open his own bank. Hamilton worried that the new Manhattan Bank would hurt business at the two banks he had founded, the Bank of New York and the New York branch of the Bank of the United States. And it did.

Hamilton passed his low opinion of Burr along to anyone who would listen. How could he know that a dinner guest would repeat his remarks in a letter that would find its way into a newspaper?

Enraged, Burr demanded that Hamilton apologize for the public insult, explain what he had said, or deny everything. Hamilton refused. A proud man, he was defensive about his humble beginnings, and he'd always fought being backed into a corner, even if a duel was the outcome. Letters passed between the two men. In one of them, Hamilton wrote: "I trust, on more reflection, you will see the matter in the same light with me. If not, I can only regret the circumstance and must abide by the consequences."

Burr would probably have agreed with Hamilton when he said that they had "always behaved with courtesy to each other." But courteous or not, Burr very definitely did not see the matter in the "same light" as Hamilton. As for the "consequences," in June 1804 Burr challenged Hamilton to a duel.

Duels were common among military officers as a badge of courage and leadership, and General Alexander Hamilton and Colonel Aaron Burr were both military men. Hamilton had been involved in six duels as a challenger or as a second, but he had never actually dueled. Even knowing what terrible pain the dueling death of his son had caused his family, he accepted Burr's challenge.

With a wife, seven children, and large debts left over from building the Grange, Hamilton had more to lose than Burr. After all, Burr was a widower with one child happily married and living far away. But neither he nor Burr told family or friends of their plans.

It goes without saying, however, that the duel was very much on Hamilton's mind. He told his second, Nathaniel Pendleton, that he planned to fire his gun in the air. He even wrote that he was going "to *reserve* and *throw away* my first fire and *I have thoughts* even of *reserving* my second fire and thus giving a double opportunity to Col Burr to pause and reflect."

Hamilton's last concern was for his family and the future of his adopted country. Though he wrote his will and finished up his legal cases, he spent most of the two weeks before the duel at the Grange with his family and close friends, even making a call on ailing Robert Troup. Last of all, he penned a long and loving letter to Eliza to be opened in case of his death.

Alexander Hamilton slept in his New York town house the night before the duel. He woke at 3:00 A.M. to give himself time to write a hymn dedicated to his wife. Just as he finished, he heard a knock on the door. It was Nathaniel Pendleton and Dr. David Hosack.

It was time to cross the river to Weehawken.

Chapter 9

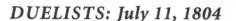

DUELISTS: *July 11, 1804*

At exactly 7:00 *A.M., Alexander Hamilton and Aaron* Burr stepped to one side of the dueling ground as Hamilton's second, Nathaniel Pendleton, and Burr's second, William Van Ness, drew lots to decide where the duelists would stand. Though Pendleton won, he and Hamilton made a strange decision. They chose the north side. Because of the angle of the ledge, Hamilton would be facing the low morning sun that reflected off the river. That gave Burr the advantage of having the sun behind him, which made his opponent clearly visible.

Pendleton and Van Ness drew lots again, this time to decide which one would supervise the duel. Once again, Pendleton was the winner. The two men then paced off ten steps, and Hamilton and Burr took their positions.

Because Burr had been the challenger, Hamilton had the choice of weapons. He had chosen the same flintlock pistols that his son Philip had used in his fatal duel three years before. Each pistol weighed several pounds and used large lead bullets.

The seconds loaded the pistols and cocked them with a click that sounded loud in the morning stillness. Van Ness gave Burr his pistol, but Pendleton hesitated. He asked Hamilton if he wanted the hair trigger set, which would cause the gun to fire more quickly.

"Not this time," Hamilton replied.

Handing over the cocked pistol, Pendleton then recited the rules. He would ask if the two men were ready. If they were, he would say *"Present"* and they would fire. If only one duelist fired, he would wait for his opponent's second to count "One, two, three, fire." His opponent could then return fire.

Burr and Hamilton stood sideways to each other. They both placed their right foot about two feet in front of their left and turned their heads over their right shoulders, standard dueling posture that offered as narrow a target as possible. But when Pendleton asked if they were ready, Hamilton was not. Sunlight sparkling off the river bothered him.

"Stop," he ordered. "In certain states of light one requires glasses." He pulled a pair of spectacles from his pocket and put them on with one hand while aiming his pistol in several directions with the other. "This will do," he said. "Now you may proceed."

When Pendleton again asked if they were ready, both men responded that they were.

"Present."

The two men lifted their pistols and fired—a split second apart. Burr's bullet tore into Hamilton's stomach above his right hip, while Hamilton's bullet struck four feet from Burr, shattering a tree branch twelve feet above the ground.

Burr's second, William Van Ness, always insisted that Hamilton was the first to fire. For the rest of his life, Hamilton's second, Nathaniel Pendleton, claimed that Burr had fired first and that Hamilton's shot was a reflex action after the bullet had already struck him. There was no debate as to whether or not Hamilton was hit. He stretched up to his full height, twisted to the left, and fell to the ground in agony. "I am a dead man," he gasped.

Pandemonium followed.

Pendleton ran to the top of the footpath. "Dr. Hosack!" he shouted.

Burr stepped toward the wounded man, but Van Ness stopped him. If the duel was later taken to court, Dr. Hosack could testify that he had seen Burr. Opening an umbrella, Van Ness shaded Burr's face as the two of them hurried down the footpath before Dr. Hosack came up.

Just as Burr and his second climbed aboard their barge, Burr cried out, "I must go and speak to him." Eager to keep Burr from returning to the bloody scene, Van Ness ran back up the path to check out the situation himself.

Dr. Hosack had arrived on the ledge to find Hamilton in Pendleton's arms, on the grass half sitting against a boulder. The doctor examined the wounded man. The bullet had fractured a rib, gone through his liver, and lodged in his spine. Dr. Hosack, Pendleton, and the oarsmen carried Hamilton down the path and made him as comfortable as they could in the bottom of the barge.

They pushed off.

As they crossed the Hudson River in the bright sunlight on what would soon become a hot July day, Hamilton opened his eyes. "My vision is indistinct," he mumbled. Then he whispered, "Take care of that pistol. It may go off and do harm. Pendleton knows that I did not intend to fire at him." Apparently he didn't remember pulling the trigger.

Hamilton, who was semiconscious and could no longer feel his legs, didn't speak again. With everyone in a state of shock, no one else spoke either. The only sound was the steady creak of the oarlocks and the slap of the oars in the water as the oarsmen rowed as hard and as fast as they could. As they approached the same dock they had left only hours before, Hamilton spoke of his wife. "Let the event be gradually broken to her, but give her hopes," he murmured.

Hamilton's friend William Bayard stood at the end of his dock watching the barge approach. When he saw how serious Hamilton's wound was, he burst into tears and sent his servants to fetch a cot. Placing Hamilton on the cot, the servants carried him up to a second-floor bedroom in Bayard's home.

Forty-nine-year-old General Alexander Hamilton died at 2:00 P.M. the next day, July 12, 1804, surrounded by his large and loving family.

National shock and outrage greeted the news of Hamilton's death. Boston and Philadelphia went into mourning for "the first of their fellow citizens." But it was New York City that suffered the greatest pain. "The feelings of the whole community are agonized beyond description," grieved Oliver Wolcott, Jr., who had served as Washington's secretary of the treasury after Hamilton resigned.

A state funeral for New York's most prominent citizen was held on July 14, 1804. New Yorkers wore black bands on their arms, all businesses were closed, church bells tolled, and ships in the harbor flew their flags at half-mast. To the roll of muffled drums, militia units led the funeral procession through New York's downtown streets to Trinity Church.

Hamilton's riderless horse, with the general's empty boots and spurs reversed in the stirrups, was led behind eight pallbearers carrying the casket. Hamilton's four oldest sons and representatives from every profession and level of New York society came next, with the somber procession taking two hours to pass the thousands of weeping New Yorkers who filled the streets and rooftops.

Following the moving ceremony in Trinity Church, the casket was interred in the Trinity churchyard. After the casket was lowered into the grave, the militia troops formed a square around the grave and fired three volleys into the air. The full military honors bestowed on Alexander Hamilton were surely a fitting farewell for the orphaned fourteen-year-old boy who long ago had craved to make a name for himself in war.

Epilogue

Aaron Burr was indicted for murder of Alexander Hamilton in New Jersey and indicted for a lesser crime or a misdemeanor in New York. To avoid arrest, he fled. For the next few months he traveled, first to Philadelphia and then through the South. After visiting his daughter in South Carolina, Burr arrived in Washington in November 1804. "We are, indeed, fallen on evil times," lamented one senator as Vice President Burr, still the acting president of the Senate, presided over the Senate's opening session.

Burr, who continued to preside over the Senate until his term as vice-president was up the following year, also presided at the impeachment trial of Supreme Court Justice Samuel Chase. But Burr was out in the cold when George Clinton was sworn in as Thomas Jefferson's new vice president on March 4, 1805.

With a scheme that he'd been concocting for years, in the spring of 1805, Burr toured what was then considered the West: Kentucky, Tennessee, Ohio, Indiana Territory, Mississippi Territory, and New Orleans. On his travels he met up with General James Wilkinson, commander of the United States army, Senator Jonathan Dayton of New Jersey, and wealthy, idealistic Harman Blennerhassett. The four men plotted to organize an expedition to conquer Louisiana and form a new empire that would include all of the western states. Although the details of the conspiracy are still not fully known, it is believed that annexing Mexico was part of their plan.

As supporters rallied around Burr, President Jefferson took note of the rumors of treason that had begun to circulate. In July 1806, Burr wrote a letter in code to General Wilkinson outlining the plot. But aware that they would all be hung for treason if their expedition failed, General Wilkinson panicked. To save his own neck, he turned Burr's coded letter over to President Jefferson. With proof in hand, Jefferson ended the conspiracy.

After several arrests, close calls, and court appearances, Burr escaped into the Virginia wilderness. He was captured in February 1807 and brought to trial on charges of treason in Richmond, Virginia. Determined as President Jefferson was to have Burr convicted, the Constitution clearly defines what a treasonous act is. Because those guidelines couldn't be met, Burr was acquitted and set free.

After enduring a year of public anger and death threats, Burr fled to Europe. Forever resolute, he tried to raise foreign money to establish his western American empire, but there were no takers. Four years later, Burr returned to New York and his law practice.

In 1812, Burr learned that his only grandchild had fallen ill and died. A few months later, his daughter, Theodosia, was lost at sea. Just as Burr had been doubly orphaned as a boy, he once again suffered a double loss.

After a brief marriage to a wealthy widow, Eliza Jumel, eighty-year-old

Aaron Burr died on September 14, 1836, in a New York hotel. In contrast to the citywide mourning at Alexander Hamilton's funeral and his burial with military honors in New York's Trinity Church, Aaron Burr was buried in a simple ceremony near his father's and grandfather's graves in Princeton, New Jersey.

Bibliography

The Annals of America. Vols. 2, 3, 4. Chicago: Encyclopedia Britannica, Inc., 1976.

Athearn, Robert G. *The American Heritage New Illustrated History of the United States.* Vol. 4, *A New Nation.* New York: Dell Publishing Co., Inc., 1963.

Bobbé, Dorothie. "The Boyhood of Alexander Hamilton." *American Heritage*, Vol. VI, No. 4 (June 1955), pp. 4–9; 96–99.

Brookhiser, Richard. *Alexander Hamilton: American.* New York: The Free Press, 1999.

Chernow, Ron. *Alexander Hamilton.* New York: Penguin Press, 2004.

Chidsey, Donald Barr. *The Great Conspiracy.* New York: Crown Publishers, Inc., 1967.

Daniels, Jonathan. *Ordeal of Ambition: Jefferson, Hamilton, Burr.* Garden City, N.Y.: Doubleday & Company, Inc., 1970.

Davis, Matthew L. *Memoirs of Aaron Burr with Miscellaneous Selections from His Correspondence.* Vol. I. Boston, Massachusetts: Indy Publisher, no date.

Editors of *American Heritage. The American Heritage Book of the Presidents and Famous Americans.* Vol. I, *George Washington and John Adams.* New York: Dell Publishing Co., Inc., 1967.

Flexner, James Thomas. *The Traitor and the Spy.* New York: Harcourt, Brace and Company, 1953.

———. *The Young Hamilton: A Biography.* Boston: Little, Brown and Company, 1978.

Hamilton, Alexander. *Writings.* New York: The Library of America, 2001.

Isenberg, Nancy. *Fallen Founder: The Life of Aaron Burr.* New York: Viking, 2007.

Jackson, Kenneth T., and Valerie Paley. "History Makers: A Conversation with Ron Chernow." *The New-York Journal of American History,* No. 3 (Spring 2004), pp. 59–65.

Kennedy, Roger G. *Burr, Hamilton, and Jefferson: A Study in Character.* New York: Oxford University Press, 2000.

Lomask, Milton. *Aaron Burr: The Conspiracy and Years of Exile, 1805–1836.* New York: Farrar, Straus and Giroux, 1982.

———. *Aaron Burr: The Years from Princeton to Vice President, 1756–1805.* New York: Farrar, Straus and Giroux, 1979.

McCullough, David. *1776.* New York: Simon & Schuster, 2005.

Pearson, Michael. "The Siege of Quebec, 1775–1776." *American Heritage,* Vol. XXIII, No. 2 (February 1972), pp. 8–15; 104–8.

Randall, Willard Sterne. "Why Benedict Arnold Did It." *American Heritage,* Vol. XLI, No. 6 (September/October 1990), pp. 60–73.

Roberts, Kenneth, ed. *March to Quebec: Journals of the Members of Arnold's Expedition.* New York: Doubleday, Doran & Company, Inc., 1938.

Rogow, Arnold A. *A Fatal Friendship. Alexander Hamilton and Aaron Burr.* New York: Hill and Wang, 1998.

St. George, Judith. *John and Abigail Adams: An American Love Story.* New York: Holiday House, 2001.

———. *Mason and Dixon's Line of Fire.* New York: G. P. Putnam's Sons, 1991.

Vail, Philip. *The Great American Rascal: The Turbulent Life of Aaron Burr.* New York: Hawthorn Books, Inc., 1973.

Wandell, Samuel H., and Meade Minngerode. *Aaron Burr.* Vol. Two. New York: G. P. Putnam's Sons, 1925.

Webb, James R. "The Eternal Encounter." *American Heritage,* Vol. XXVI, No. 5 (August 1975), pp. 45–52; 92–93.

Index